THE MYSTERY OF MARKET MOVEMENTS

Since 1996, Bloomberg Press has published books for financial professionals on investing, economics, and policy affecting investors. Titles are written by leading practitioners and authorities, and have been translated into more than 20 languages.

The Bloomberg Financial Series provides both core reference knowledge and actionable information for financial professionals. The books are written by experts familiar with the work flows, challenges, and demands of investment professionals who trade the markets, manage money, and analyze investments in their capacity of growing and protecting wealth, hedging risk, and generating revenue.

For a list of available titles, please visit our Web site at www.wiley.com/go/bloombergpress.

THE MYSTERY OF MARKET MOVEMENTS

An Archetypal Approach
to Investment Forecasting
and Modelling

Niklas Hageback

BLOOMBERG PRESS
An Imprint of
WILEY

Other Wiley Editorial Offices
John Wiley & Sons, 111 River Street, Hoboken, NJ 07030, USA
John Wiley & Sons, The Atrium, Southern Gate, Chichester, West Sussex, P019 8SQ, United Kingdom
John Wiley & Sons (Canada) Ltd., 5353 Dundas Street West, Suite 400, Toronto, Ontario, M9B 6HB, Canada
John Wiley & Sons Australia Ltd., 42 McDougall Street, Milton, Queensland 4064, Australia
Wiley-VCH, Boschstrasse 12, D-69469 Weinheim, Germany

ISBN 978-1-118-84498-4 (Hardcover)
ISBN 978-1-118-84499-1 (ePDF)
ISBN 978-1-118-84500-4 (ePub)
ISBN 978-1-118-90454-1 (oBook)

Typeset in 11/13pt, AGaramondPro-Regular by Thomson Digital, Noida, India.

Printed in Singapore by Markono Print Media Pte Ltd.

10 9 8 7 6 5 4 3 2 1

Contents

Acknowledgments

I wish to express my gratitude to Cherry Cheng Ka-Wing and Daniel Kongo Hedblom for their contributions to the background research.

I would also like to thank Nick Wallwork, Kimberly Monroe-Hill, and Emilie Herman from John Wiley & Sons as well as Stephen Isaacs from Bloomberg Press for their help with publishing and editing.

Introduction

> *"Experience teaches us no less clearly than reason, that men believe themselves free, simply because they are conscious of their actions, and unconscious of the causes whereby those actions are determined."*
> —Baruch Spinoza, "Part III: On the Origin and Nature of the Emotions; Postulates (Proposition II, Note)" from R. H. M. Elwes, trans., *The Ethics*, 1955, p. 54 (original work published 1677)

In the wake of the dot-com crash and the collapse of the US housing bubble, it is clear that non-rational impulses, such as the mania at the height of these bubbles and the subsequent panics that followed in the downturns, play a major part in collective human investment behaviour. These irrational sentiments, which have the capacity to greatly influence asset prices and at times feed financial bubbles that threaten to trigger great social unrest, have been given many names. The founding father of fundamental analysis, Ben Graham, and later his most famous disciple, the investor Warren Buffett, named them the manic-depressive *Mr. Market*; the economist J. M. Keynes referred to *animal spirits*; and the former US Federal Reserve chairman Alan Greenspan talked about *irrational exuberance*.

The inability of conventional economics to account for human irrationality renders the commonly accepted economic and financial theories void. Economists adhering to these conformist thoughts are at a loss as to how to adapt their theories to account for collective human behaviour that does not follow the "rational man" assumption. To date no one has been able to pinpoint and explain the mechanics of these forces, other than relating to them in anecdotal fashion or quickly glossing them over as an unknown variable.

Consequently, interest is, and has been, growing in developing alternative approaches to economic theory, such as *behavioural finance*. However, these newer concepts have proved uneven at best in predicting and explaining financial bubbles. They all fail to answer the two key questions: When and why are financial bubbles likely to form?

Given the dramatic impact such irrational fluctuations can have on asset prices, and on society at large, and the recognised, but generally overlooked, inability of fundamental valuation models to factor them in, it is vital that we identify the underlying drivers. Existing theory has proved incapable of doing so, but there is a way. However, to understand it, we must first delve into psychology and explore the collective unconscious and its archetypes—innate mental images that exist unconsciously in us all and affect our behaviour and judgment without our being consciously aware of it.

Recent developments in neuroscience have brought greater understanding of the workings of the brain and how it relates to the much more elusive concept of the mind. There has been a fundamental shift from the position that nurture is basically responsible for human development and behaviour, in other words, everyone is starting with a blank slate, to an acceptance and understanding of the powerful influence nature holds. Modern research supports the existence of an unconscious, with a part operating at a collective level, impacting societal movements, whether in fashion, political trends, even social unrest and revolutions—and the financial markets. Individually or collectively, human choices, including investment decisions, are affected to a large degree by the prevailing social mood or *zeitgeist*. The collective unconscious plays an important role in creating and directing these social mood swings.

The term *collective unconscious* was coined by the Swiss psychologist Carl Gustav Jung (1875–1961) early in the twentieth century during a period in which he was collaborating with his Austrian contemporary Sigmund Freud (1856–1939). Jung's thinking on the collective unconscious and its archetypes came over time to gain broad acceptance among the psychology profession and academics. Jung incorporated Freud's model of the unconscious, what Jung called the *personal unconscious*, but he proposed the existence of a second, far deeper form of the unconscious lying under the personal—the collective unconscious, where the archetypes reside. The personal unconscious comprises an individual's experiences that have been forgotten or suppressed into the unconscious. It is unique to each person. The collective unconscious, on the other hand, contains psychic material—the archetypes—common to mankind and therefore universal and impersonal throughout time and regardless of cultural context.

Archetypes can be seen as mental structures or thought patterns that through mankind's history have become hard-coded into our DNA. The purpose of archetypes is to support the mind's objective to maintain a holistic equilibrium in order to avoid the risk of neurotic collective behaviour; in a sense, it is a psychological survival instinct functioning on an all-encompassing human level. When activated by events or emotions that disturb the balance of the mind, such as pent-up aggressions not allowed by the conscious due to prevailing norms or moral conventions in society or the need for a release of self-reflection, archetypal forces begin to well up into the conscious in order to restore the mind's equilibrium.

There are many different archetypes, although not an infinite number. Some archetypes have the nature of a character, such as The Great Mother or The Warrior; others are related to situations typical to mankind, such as Birth or Death, or to an object, such as the Moon, the Sword, or Fire. Archetypes are comprehensive, timeless, and static, and appear in all cultures, though their manifestations can vary in different settings and time epochs. They are innate and as such are passed genetically from generation to generation.

As archetypes reside in the collective unconscious, the only tangible footprints from which they can be observed are in the form of symbols. These symbols could be specific words or expressions that seemingly spontaneously appear in our dialogue, or images that appear in our dreams. The level of frequency of their appearance indicates the urgency, the need, for the archetype to be expressed and begin to impact our thinking.

The triggering of an archetype such as The Warrior, by the suppression in the conscious of aggressive tendencies, for example, could give rise to the use of war-like metaphors in non-war-like contexts. War-related words could emerge in descriptions of sport—they invaded the pitch, the home team massacred the opposition—or as cultural trends, such as a sudden crop of war-related movies, or a fad for uniforms in fashion. At first, such metaphors are adapted and used by the collective community without awareness of the activation of a war-like archetype and the need by the mind to increase aggressive thinking to restore a holistic mind. The spread of such language and worldview can trigger heightened levels of aggression in society which increase the likelihood for riots and even wars, and would in the financial markets lead to excessive risk taking. And when such actions manifest, The Warrior archetype has fulfilled its purpose because it has helped restore the equilibrium in the mind, and it starts to recede and eventually becomes dormant again in the unconscious. Other societal examples of archetypes at work include the sexual repression of the Victorian era, which emerged as the hysteria and neurotic behaviour commonly displayed by women of the era. This of course flowed through into fashion, with even grand pianos affected—dressed with curtains to hide the curvaceous legs so scandalously suggestive of womanly contours and likely to inspire impure thoughts. In the 1950s, the witch hunts and reds-under-the-bed paranoia of McCarthyism was another archetypal expression. As a simple rule of thumb, to identify the types of archetypes likely to be at work is to understand and pin down the existing taboos of the era.

When studying archetypal activation through its tangible manifestations, symbols, it is important to distinguish symbols from signs. Whereas a symbol contains an unconscious element of meaning, a sign just has the one meaning, like a stop sign means stop and nothing else. Through the study of symbols we see that people often say or write one thing and do or mean something completely different; this is what happens when the archetype is beginning to move from the unconscious into the conscious, without the person being aware of its impact on their thoughts and behaviour, or its wider, collective effect in altering the mood of society, or zeitgeist.

The emergence of the language of the archetypes and through its shifts, the symbols, whether in speech, literature, dreams, art, or photography, signals when the zeitgeist is about to change. They appear before the thought pattern leads to a change in behaviour. So by watching for these direct pipelines into the collective unconscious, one is able to tap into the developing zeitgeist and predict future trends, be they cultural or political—or investment behaviour. Whereas influences of archetypes and the unconscious have been studied on a number of mainly individual but also some collective human endeavours, very little, if any, research has been conducted on the potential impact of the collective unconscious on trends in the financial markets.

Recent advances in text analysis and text-mining techniques have been a boon for the advancement of the study of archetype-related symbols. Huge banks of global information, or Big Data, are now easily available for analysis via the Internet. Claims and theories previously considered "intangible," such as the Jungian archetypes, and previously described in abstract terms, can now be defined and verified. Financial markets, with their extensive output and frequent updates of real-time data, provide fertile ground for statistical testing of the archetype hypothesis. By building a record of the appearance of archetypal symbols and analysing the frequency of their appearance versus financial indexes, one can attempt to predict price trends over time.

With this context in mind, the aim of this book is to demonstrate the workings of the collective unconscious and provide an empirically verified measurement methodology designed to capture the subliminal forces that influence human behaviour and in particular investment decisions, thereby demonstrating how archetypes can give rise to financial bubbles. Through exploring the collective unconscious and using symbol analysis to quantify the impact of archetypal forces on human thought and behaviour, we can predict turns in markets and develop strategies to profit from them.

The generic features of the statistical tracking of archetype-related symbols also accommodate further research in other applicable areas of finance and deliver a new tool for use in fields such as political science, consumer behaviour, and marketing.

This book is written for anyone with an interest in:

- Behavioural finance with a focus on modelling and forecasting.
- Psychology with a highlight on how archetypes and associated symbols influence collective societal behaviour.
- Linguistics, especially text analytics and data-mining techniques.

The *Mystery of Market Movements* is structured in 10 chapters:

- **Chapter 1: "Psychology: A Primer"** gives an overview and history of psychology to provide a context of where the unconscious fits in. It also discusses the millennia-long difficulties in pinning down exact definitions of key psychological concepts, such as consciousness and the mind. In addition, Chapter 1 gives an introduction to the concepts of the unconscious and Sigmund Freud's theories of the mind.
- **Chapter 2: "Archetypes and Symbols"** introduces Carl Jung's view of the collective unconscious and its archetypes and how they relate to Freud's ideas. It also discusses the circumstances required for archetypes to activate and the symbols that are the tangible manifestations of archetypes and thus can be deployed for measurement purposes.
- **Chapter 3: "How Archetypes Influence and Impact Behaviour"** highlights archetypal causations to phenomena such as zeitgeist, scapegoats, and hysteria in society.
- **Chapter 4: "Archetypal Influences in the Financial Markets"** provides examples of how archetypes cause financial bubbles.
- **Chapter 5: "Existing Approaches to Capture Sentiments in Financial Markets, and Why They Do Not Work"** gives a critique of the current financial forecasting models.
- **Chapter 6: "Developing a Conceptual Measurement Methodology Based on Archetypal Forces: Part I: Building Blocks"** discusses the building blocks, a highlight of the components that constitute the measurement units of the model.

- **Chapter 7: "Developing a Conceptual Measurement Methodology Based on Archetypal Forces: Part II: The Data"** gives data sources, provides a review of the requirements for suitable data sources, and includes samples of how the symbol selection is conducted.
- **Chapter 8: "Developing a Conceptual Measurement Methodology Based on Archetypal Forces: Part III: The Model"** provides the model and a step-by-step guide that gives insights on the statistical methods applied to develop and test archetypal symbol time series.
- **Chapter 9: "Examples of Archetypal Influences on the Formation of Financial Bubbles"** demonstrates the connection between specific archetypes and the dot-com bubble and US property bubble.
- **Chapter 10: "Conclusion."**

The first two chapters give an introduction to the key concepts of psychology and its broader context, namely the unconscious and the archetypes that underpin the measurement methodology. Chapters 3 to 9 demonstrate archetypal manifestations in society in general and the financial markets in particular. These chapters also discuss existing models to forecast investor sentiments and their flaws and proposes a methodology for measuring and testing the forecasting capabilities of the fluctuation of archetypal symbols and their impact on financial asset prices. Recent bubbles are highlighted, and the influences of specific archetypes are discussed, as well as open areas of research.

Supplementing the book is a dedicated website, www.forecastrix.com, that presents continuously updated bespoke archetypal indexes with predictive capabilities to major financial indexes. The website will enable readers to track changes in archetypal mood patterns and enhance their investment decisions. The website also includes colour versions of the black-and-white figures appearing in this book.

CHAPTER 1

Psychology: A Primer

Human reflections on psychology are as old as mankind; however, these reflections evolved into a more structured form once our ancestors could contextualise them as either part of religion, philosophy, or medicine. The oldest surviving document that can be linked to psychology as an abstract idea—a scripture prescribing medical remedies for diseases induced by demons—comes from ancient Egypt.[1] Later, the Greek philosopher Aristotle (384 BC–322 BC) examined various psychological abstractions from a philosophical perspective in his treatise *De Anima* (On the Soul).[2] His Greek contemporary Plato (427 BC–347 BC) introduced the notion of the soul as a separate entity from the body, a concept that remains the subject of debate to this day. And the language of Aristotle and Plato gave us the word *psychology*, its root being the ancient Greek for "the study of the soul."[3]

In Western civilisation up to the mid-1800s, the main exercise of psychology was in the study of the soul from a Christian theological perspective, its relationship to the human body, and its fate in the afterlife.[4] It was not until the 1870s that psychology became a standalone academic discipline, when the German physician Wilhelm Wundt (1832–1920) developed scientific principles for the study of the mind. Wundt set up a laboratory to study the mind through a range of empirical tests, such as by timing responses to various stimuli. In 1874, he published the first textbook on psychology, *Grundzüge der Physiologischen Psychologie* (*Principles of Physiological Psychology*).[5]

Since Wilhelm Wundt's days, psychology has evolved rapidly via academic research and practice and is defined today as *the study of the mind and behaviour*[6]—the mind being all mental processes, including thoughts, perceptions, and memories, and behaviour being all observable actions and reactions, including speech and bodily movements. Given the breadth of the subject, psychology can be approached from different angles, including the following key approaches[7]:

- **Behavioural**—Responses learned through classical conditioning, as demonstrated by Pavlov's dogs, or operant conditioning (the use of reinforcement or punishment to alter behaviour).
- **Cognitive**—Highlights the parts of psychology covering memory, intelligence, perception, thought processes, problem solving, language, and learning.
- **Biopsychological**—The influence of hormones, brain structures, chemicals, and diseases on behaviour. Human behaviour is seen as a direct result of bodily conditions.
- **Evolutionary**—The biological bases for what are considered universal mental characteristics and behaviours and how through natural selection these can be distinguished.
- **Humanistic**—Focuses on human potential and motivation, including the questions of free will and *self-actualisation*, the psychological drive to realise one's talents and potentials.
- **Psychodynamic**—The role of the unconscious mind and its impact on conscious behaviour. The psychodynamic aspect also covers the influence of childhood experiences and developmental issues.

Despite long debate, in some cases over millenia, there is still no consensus on the exact definitions of many key concepts of psychology; this includes areas such as consciousness, instincts, the mind, the soul, and free will. Not only do definitions differ depending on school of thought but the definitions are sometimes even overlapping or interchangeable. It is ironic that notions so critical to describing our human make-up are still so hard to define. Is the mind a set of chemical processes in the brain or is it something more abstract? The loose definitions cause confusion and have hampered progress in research. However, it is important to have a grasp of the fundamental components of the psychological constitution and their definitions, albeit loose, before examining the workings of the collective unconsciousness. This chapter will provide highlights of psychology as an academic discipline and give insights to some key concepts. The reader will need to be familiar with these concepts before we discuss the archetypes and their influence on collective behaviour and, in particular, price trends in the financial markets.

Some Key Psychological Concepts

The Mind

The mind can be defined as "the collective conscious and unconscious processes in a sentient organism that direct and influence mental and physical behavior"[8]—the elements of sentience being the brain, nerve processes, cognition, and the motor and sensory processes.

It is commonly accepted that the mind, or *psyche*, possesses such attributes as perception, reason, imagination, memory, emotion, attention, and a faculty for communication. But its exact traits remain the subject of academic debate and have yet to be precisely pinned down by science. Some argue that only "higher" intellectual functions, in particular, reason, imagination, and memory, constitute the mind while emotions, such as love, hate, fear, and joy, are of a more instinctual character and not part of the mind. Others hold that rational and emotional states cannot be so distinctly separated, as their origins are shared, so both are considered to be part of the mind. Despite centuries of exploration through philosophy, religion, and psychology, a crisp definition of the mind, with objective, verifiable characteristics, eludes us. But one pivotal point has been established, as there is marked evidence for it: the mind has both a conscious and an unconscious part.[9]

The question of whether the mind and brain are one and the same, or whether the mind is somehow separate from physical existence, has been debated since the days of Plato. Three schools of thought exist: the *dualistic*, which considers the mind to exist independently of the brain; the *idealistic*, which means that only mental phenomena exist; and the *materialist*, in which the mind is the result of activities of the brain.[10] Where the psychologists and philosophers have failed, over the last decade, neuroscientists and geneticists are taking their turn at trying to define the mind, by examining the brain's electrochemical processes and genetic code. This is bringing the materialist concept of the body-mind relationship to the fore. Brain-scanning technology, such as electroencephalography (EEG) and functional magnetic resonance imaging (fMRI), has enabled neuroscience to reveal relationships between the brain and the mind. The study of patients with brain damage shows that injuries to specific parts of the brain result in specific impairments in functions seen as part of the mind. Experiments with drugs have also revealed brain-mind links; for example, sedatives reduce awareness, while stimulants do the opposite. The chemical neurotransmitter *serotonin* has been shown to have an essential role in the activity of the brain. But the advances in neuroscience and genetics have not yet provided a comprehensive picture of how the brain produces, and relates to, various functions of the mind. For example, the neuroscientific view is unable to explain emotions in terms of brain structure and processes.[11]

Consciousness

Consciousness suffers from the same vagueness of definition as does *mind*. The *Macmillan Dictionary of Psychology* describes *consciousness* as "the having of perceptions, thoughts, and feelings; awareness." Many fall into the trap of equating consciousness with self-consciousness—to be conscious it is only necessary to be aware of the external world.[12] Common synonyms for consciousness are *awareness* and *self*, and *consciousness* is often used to mean "the mind," and vice versa.

On a philosophical level, intellectuals wrestle with the metaphysical nature of the conscious. As with the concept of the mind, should consciousness be thought of as separate mental and physical states? Does it exist only in humans, or can animals possess it? Could computers or robots develop a conscious mind, and how would you recognise it?[13]

Medically, consciousness is defined as the sum of the electrical discharges occurring throughout the nervous system of a being at any given instant.[14] The important issue from the medical perspective is the amount of consciousness, and this can be expressed in a standardised gradation from full alertness to coma to brain death, and there are many techniques to measure brain activity. Among them, EEGs measure electrical activity of the brain and, through measuring the brain's oxygen consumption, provide a proxy reading of the level of neuronal activity and clues to which conscious functions are active.

One of the big mysteries of the conscious is the so-called *binding problem*: How do the different areas of the brain that receive and process information bind it together into a conscious unity and make sense of it? How does the brain bind together the colour blue and the shape circle into a blue circle, given that the processes that determine colours and shapes of objects are distinctly separate and occur in different areas of the brain. As well as being a neuroscientific question, it also holds philosophical implications: Is there an "inner man" within us binding all experiences from the different senses into awareness, or perhaps an external force that binds the experiences of all of us into a collective unconscious?[15]

Despite extensive research, no conclusive evidence has yet been produced to document the existence of animal consciousness.[16]

With regard to machines, the English mathematician Alan Turing (1912–1954), who invented one of the forerunners of the modern computer, designed a test in 1950 to determine machine consciousness. The gist of the *Turing Test*, as it became known, is that if a computer can imitate a human well enough to fool the assessors, this would be evidence of consciousness. Although there are philosophical objections to this test, it is generally seen as a valid criterion. But after more than 60 years of research and testing, and with *artificial consciousness* evolving into a research discipline in its own right, a machine has yet to satisfy the test.[17]

As highlighted previously, many questions on the boundaries of the conscious mind, as well as its function, remain unanswered; however, as will be seen in the coming sections, we are able to distinguish the conscious part of the mind from the unconscious part.

Instincts, Drives, and Reflexes

The concept of instinct has evolved since it was introduced into the field of psychology by Wilhelm Wundt in the 1870s. Initially, most repetitive behaviour was considered instinctual. However, as the understanding of instincts developed, especially after the distinguishing of the differences between animal and human instincts, it has become rare for instincts to be used in explaining human behaviour.

In the 1960s, the American psychologist Abraham Maslow (1908–1970) argued that humans do not have instincts, as evidenced by the fact that we are able to override them. Citing the maternal instinct and the survival instinct, Maslow pointed out that some women deliberately choose not to have children, that some mothers suffering depression kill their own children, and that some people choose to commit suicide. Maslow felt that although the overriding of such instincts often coincided with mental illness, humans' ability to deliberately interfere with these instincts diluted the concept of human instincts. He and his contemporaries saw instincts rather as strong biological tendencies and motivators for certain human behaviour, but they distinguished them from (animal) instincts and referred to them as *drives*.[18]

The diminished role of instincts as an explanation for human behaviour coincided with the scientific debate on *nature versus nurture*, which was especially prominent after World War II with Nazi science and referral to euthanasia fresh in mind. Thus, the scientific community's views shifted towards nurture as the preferred explanatory model of human behaviour, while concepts such as instinct and other innate patterns became politically incorrect in certain circles. Therefore, over the last 60 years, a noticeable downplaying of biological grounding has taken place in terms of explaining human behaviour but, as noted, this may have been motivated by political considerations rather than empirical evidence. If anything, the most recent research supports the existence of innate abilities (or disabilities) and their impact on human performance in terms of intelligence, criminality, and other personality traits, whether that be on an individual level or grouped in genetic clusters. However, currently, the impacts are regarded on a probabilistic rather than deterministic scale. So the current view is that humans have drive, which, unlike instinct, can be overridden by the will, but, however, generally is not. The academic discipline that studies human behaviour from a biological perspective, *sociobiology*, does not consider there to be defined human instincts but rather *biological bases* for human behaviour—possibly just another word play to avoid the use of the term *instinct*, as the terms are largely synomynous."[19]

Reflexes are a simpler form of behaviour pattern than instincts or drives. The stimulus in a reflex may not even require brain activity, like the message flowing to the spinal cord and then being transmitted back, without travelling to the brain, through a path called the reflex arc[20]—for example, the involuntary kick your doctor generates when tapping your knee with a hammer.

Following is a current definition of instinct:

> Instinct is the inherent disposition of a living organism toward a particular behavior. Instincts are generally inherited patterns of responses or reactions to certain kinds of stimuli. Instinct provides a response to external stimuli, which moves an organism to action, unless overridden by intelligence, which is creative and more versatile.[21]

The Soul

The concept of the *soul* or *spirit* brings theological connotations to the description of the mind as a non-physical substance existing separately from the body (the Latin word *spiritus* means "breath"). Most religions see the soul as surviving the death of the body, and some religions, such as Buddhism, see it being reborn after death into another body. The ancient Greeks regarded the soul as the essence of a person, giving the body life and dictating individual human behaviour. But in describing human behaviour from a scientific point of view, the concept of the soul or spirit is generally avoided because it does not lend itself to empirical testing.[22]

Free Will

The question whether humans have *free will* is closely linked with the notion of the conscious. Free will is defined as "the ability to make choices free from certain kinds of constraints; constraints might be of a physical, biological, social/cultural, or psychological nature."[23]

There are two broad schools of thought arguing the existence of free will. *Determinism* contests free will with the basic assumption that present actions are caused by the past; in other words, every decision one makes is driven by preceding events, which in turn are driven by events preceding them, in a causal chain that prevents one from acting independently and exercising choice. The other school of thought is *libertarianism*, which assumes humans to be rational agents with a capacity to make free choices among alternatives.[24]

Between these opposing views are a number of variations and combinations that relax some of the more definite conditions; for example, even if causality exists, humans still have the option to choose their actions, such as at any time making the voluntary decision to end one's own life. Other variations propose predestined outcomes or goals but state that the paths to arrive there come with free choice.

The question of free will has implications that impact religious, ethical, judicial, and scientific areas. If free will can be demonstrated not to exist, can a person then be held legally and morally accountable for his actions, if these are predetermined and cannot be influenced? From a scientific viewpoint, if actions are anchored in past events, is it possible to make precise forecasts and produce statistical probabilities on predictable outcomes? This question also involves the concepts of instincts and drives: If in a certain situation strong biological motivators are triggered, albeit possible to override but with likely low probabilities, do we then have free will?

As with so many of the key concepts in psychology, the question of free will remains open and has moved from the academic areas of religion and philosophy to neuroscience and medicine.

The Unconscious

Although there is broad acceptance among psychologists and neuroscientists of the existence of an unconscious part of the mind and its ability to affect thoughts and behaviour, its exact functions and processes have yet to be pinned down and are still a subject of debate. References to various aspects of the unconscious have long been common in fictional literature and historical tradition. For example, the dramas of the ancient Greeks and the works of Shakespeare frequently involve unconscious forces, often described as "divine inspiration," influencing behaviour of the main characters. And there are many examples of similar thinking in ancient Asian cultures. The Western philosophers of the seventeenth and eighteenth centuries pondered the nature of such subliminal forces, and it was in this period that the term *unconscious* was coined.

It is important to distinguish between unconsciousness and the unconscious. Unconsciousness is a mental state during which there is little or no response to external stimuli, such as being asleep or in a coma. The unconscious, however, is defined as "processes in the mind that occur automatically and are not available to introspection, and include thought processes, memory, affect, and motivation."[25]

Initially, the unconscious was equated with unintentional actions as it coincided with the development of hypnosis in the mid-1800s and its enthusiastic exploitation on the stage. The strange and often bizarre acts of volunteers after being induced into a hypnotic state—a state in which behaviour, as it was claimed, could be dictated but about which the subject had no memory—popularised the idea that there is a part of the mind about which we are unaware but which can be spoken to and which can influence our behaviour, seemingly against our conscious will.[26] How could a hypnotist make suggestions to subjects who are apparently asleep—though a strange form of sleep in which they can open their eyes and follow instructions—if not for the existence of an unconscious with the power to control actions?

Early Thinking

The Austrian psychologist Sigmund Freud (1856–1939) greatly advanced the fledgling discipline of psychology, particularly in developing the theories of the unconscious. His early work focused on neurotic symptoms and traumatic memories. And through his interaction with patients, he arrived at the belief that an important factor in the development of neurosis, such as acting in ways not conforming to the reigning socially acceptable norms, was due to the suppression of forbidden emotions or desires. Freud regarded the unconscious as a hidden cupboard where these forbidden thoughts were shut away as they could not be erased from memory. In particular, he felt the repression of memories of sexual thoughts and fantasies from early childhood into the unconscious was a key factor in a person developing neurotic behaviour. To better understand the features of neurosis, Freud explored techniques to draw out repressed memories from the unconscious, including hypnosis and dream analysis. Eventually he developed his own method, with patients lying on a couch and being encouraged to speak their minds freely. By analysing the symbolic meaning of their relaxed ramblings, he found hints to the nature of their emotional states and neuroses. Freud referred to this technique as *psychoanalysis*, and it was to become his landmark contribution to psychology. Its aim is to draw repressed thoughts and desires back into the conscious because, according to Freud, it is then that patients can acknowledge and release the suppressed emotions and thereby eventually free themselves from neurosis.[27]

As Freud gained more insight into the workings of the mind, he concluded that it was fuelled by flows of psychic energy, which he termed *libido*. As with any energy in a closed system, the level of libido in the mind is constant. So an examination of the direction and intensity of its flow will give the psychoanalyst indications to imbalances between the conscious and the unconscious.

Initially, Freud considered the libido to be connected with mankind's sexual development and desires, but later he came to see it as flowing back and forth between the conscious and the unconscious under the influence of two innate forces. The first he called *the pleasure principle*, which triggers the impulse to seek immediate gratification of wishes and urges, not exclusively sexual ones. Freud saw the pleasure principle as the main drive of unconscious desires. The other force he called *the reality principle*. It resides in the conscious and reins in the impulses seeking immediate gratification. It suppresses socially unacceptable urges by redirecting the libido into more socially acceptable behaviour, such as artistic pursuits, through a process called *sublimation*. However, if the libido cannot be redirected towards acceptable alternative behaviours, then neurosis begins to develop.[28]

Freud's attention was first drawn to sublimation through a tale told by the German poet Heinrich Heine (1797–1856). The main character, in his childhood, found sadistic pleasure in cutting off the tails of dogs. He grew up to become a surgeon, thereby giving his socially unacceptable behaviour an acceptable, even altruistic, outlet.[29]

At the end of his career, Freud introduced another concept, *the death drive*, which represents self-destruction, and it remains among his most controversial ideas. The death drive is, for instance, considered to be the force at work when someone is "the victim of his own success." Success has come too quickly or too abundantly for the individual's view of himself, unconsciously triggering behaviour that undoes the success. A good example is the overnight millionaire created by a lottery win who, within a few years, has squandered his newfound wealth and is back to where he was before the win.[30]

Freud summed up the features of the unconscious in his 1915 essay, "The Unconscious":

> It can be contradictory; opposing feelings or wishes can coexist. For example, you can feel love and hate for the same thing at the same time;
>
> Repressed thoughts or emotions are likely to return to the conscious in some form;
>
> The unconscious is timeless; its contents have no chronological order, the cause and effect relationship can be put out of play;
>
> In people with a mental disorder, it can thrust itself into the conscious and replace physical reality with psychic reality, such as fantasies, dreams and symbolism.[31]

Freud's Picture of the Mind

Freud developed a holistic concept of the mind, the *topographical model,* to incorporate the relationship between the conscious and the unconscious[32] (see Figure 1.1). It is often depicted like an iceberg, with just the conscious mind above water level and the unconscious mind deep below. It introduces the concept of a *preconscious* residing between the conscious and the

FIGURE 1.1   Freud's Topographical Model, Depicted as an Iceberg

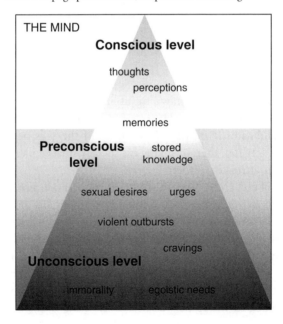

unconscious—a part of the mind whose contents are unconscious but not repressed and thus easily recalled into the conscious.

It is important to note that Freud did not believe that the conscious, preconscious, and unconscious could be pinned down to physical locations in the brain. The iceberg metaphor also highlights his view that the preconscious and unconscious comprise the largest part of the mind.

Eventually, Freud came to realise deficiencies in his topographical model, such as being too simplistic and not accurately capturing the relationships between the various parts. Consequently, he developed the vital concepts of the *id*, the *ego*, and the *super-ego* and he introduced them into a more detailed map of the mind, which he called the *structural model* (see Figure 1.2).

- The id, which is an innate function and resides in the unconscious, contains mankind's basic drives. It is a source of the libido and acts along the lines of the pleasure principle.
- The ego resides in the conscious, but partly also exists in the preconscious and unconscious. Influenced by the reality principle, it seeks to redirect drives from the id considered unacceptable.
- The super-ego is largely an unconscious function, but with parts also in the conscious and preconscious. It serves as a kind of conscience, aspiring to comply with societal norms but also the ego's ambitions, and hence has a policing function over the drives of the id.[33]

FIGURE 1.2   The Structural Model of the Mind

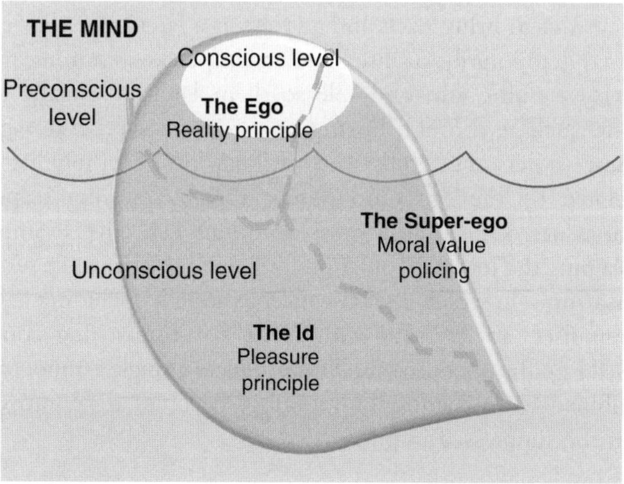

Freud's new model of the mind enabled him to explain mental disorders with greater precision. For instance, neuroses of a narcissistic nature could be identified as conflicts between the ego and the id and psychoses as conflicts between the ego and the external world.

Defense Mechanisms

The ego has a set of *defense mechanisms* it can deploy, usually at the unconscious level, to handle conflicts with the id, the super-ego, or the external environment, such as societal norms or taboos. They are usually activated to prevent mental discomfort or angst. There are a number of defense mechanisms and some with overlapping features, sometimes making them hard to precisely distinguish, but the following are the most important for understanding the collective unconscious:[34]

- **Repression**—an impulse that forces something emotionally painful to be forgotten and consigned to the unconscious. Because the psychological issue has not been dealt with or resolved by the conscious, it continues to affect the person unconsciously and can eventually develop into mental disorders. For example, a person who represses memories of abuse experienced during childhood is likely to have difficulties forming relationships until the repressed feelings have been addressed.
- **Suppression**—a conscious act to forget something, in an attempt to cope with a troubling situation. Suppression is similar to repression, but the unpleasant feelings are pushed down consciously rather than unconsciously, and to the preconscious rather than the unconscious, and are therefore easier to bring back and address at a later stage. For example, a person may temporarily suppress violent impulses stemming from being delayed by a traffic jam and release them later in socially acceptable behaviour, such as through boxing or vigorous exercise at a gym.
- **Projection**—a person or group unconsciously projects thoughts or feelings not tolerated by the ego onto others, thereby creating scapegoats for particular issues. One of the most notorious collective examples is the Nazis' blaming the Jewish population for Germany's defeat in World War I.
- **Condensation**—in which several concepts, usually including aggressive or sexual impulses, are blended with other non-threatening concepts and suppressed into the unconscious. This produces a single symbol to represent the combined components. This symbol becomes a figurative form to represent the suppressed impulses.

- **Denial**—a person or group denies reality by pretending it does not exist, like the deluded ruler and his subjects in the tale of the "Emperor's New Clothes." Examples include someone told he has a terminal illness who will initially go through a stage of denial, pretending this is not the case, before reality finally sinks in.
- **Displacement**—the redirecting of feelings or actions from a dangerous outlet to a safer one; for example, a person yelling at his secretary after being reprimanded by his boss.
- **Rationalisation**—to seek a rational explanation or justification for upsetting actions or behaviour caused by factors too unpleasant to acknowledge; for example, a person whose application for a job is rejected and who rationalises the failure by claiming he was not really that interested in the job. Another example is a student who fails a test and rationalises that it was the result of poor teaching and not his lack of preparation. Rationalisation protects the ego by avoiding or circumventing the true reason for events or behaviour, whether or not controllable.
- **Reaction formation**—the disguising of beliefs or impulses, considered unacceptable, by the exaggerated expression of opposite beliefs or impulses. For example, some men unhappily possess homosexual tendencies and suppress these tendencies; they then project instead a hatred of homosexuals, and they attack in others what they hate in themselves.
- **Regression**—the return to a previous stage of mental development in a situation of adversity, such as an adult acting childishly in response to a situation, say, by refusing to leave bed, or hiding under the blankets in bed after a bad day at work.
- **Sublimation**—the acting out of unacceptable impulses in a socially acceptable way, such as by finding outlets for the libido in cultural or intellectual pursuits.

Freudian Slippage

Sigmund Freud, always keen to promote his legacy, insisted that psychoanalysis is a science. But he was never able to produce the kind of statistical data that would have allowed his theories to be empirically tested and independently verified and as such qualify as "proper science." He usually backed the various theories he published with individual case studies and anecdotal evidence. Given the lack of robust volumes of data to analyse, another psychoanalyst reviewing the same cases could come to a different and even contradictory conclusion.

The academics of Freud's day were skeptical of his claim to have developed a science, a skepticism that has remained to this day. The Austrian philosopher Karl Popper (1902–1994) held that Freud's theories were disqualified from being considered proper scientific theories because they were "unfalsifiable"— that is, it was impossible to prove them through empirical testing. Many have attempted over the years to test Freud's theories empirically, but they have only managed, at best, to concur with his ideas in broad terms. Clinical testing provides strong scientific backing for the existence of an unconscious part of the mind, but it appears to operate differently from how Freud envisioned it, and no evidence has been found to support his abstract notions of the ego, the super-ego, or the id.[35]

Despite the reservations of contemporary science and the lack of scientific foundation, Freud's structural model still plays an influential role in describing the concept of the mind, including the unconscious and its various functions, and is often used as an educational method in introductory psychology.

Current Thinking

Psychology of today has moved away from Freud's notion of the unconscious. Each of psychology's multifaceted disciplines has its own doctrine and focus of research regarding the unconscious. In cognitive psychology, researchers are studying *implicit memory*—a type of memory in which previous experiences aid in the performing of a task without conscious awareness of these previous experiences. Psychologists have been investigating *priming* and *automaticity*, the ability to do something without being actively aware of it, such as repetitive menial tasks (for example, riding a bicycle).

Another area of research involves the *unconscious acquisition of information*. While a person is not consciously aware of himself absorbing information, these processes can still influence behaviour and decision-making processes. Empirical tests have shown that a person can act on information that was processed only in the unconscious *before* any awareness of that information or decision to act enters the conscious, for example, unconsciously determining patterns of sequences for various events. In tests, such as detecting the frequency of certain cards recurring in a deck of cards being displayed, subjects asked to pay specific attention to particular types of events and estimate their frequency are rarely able to provide better estimates than subjects given no hint beforehand of what they are to be asked to do.[36]

Another perspective is on *unconscious mental processes*. Studies show aspects of the unconscious influencing a number of cognitive processes, including decision making, something which has been extensively researched and invested in by the advertising industry. For instance, applying visual subliminal stimuli to promote sales for certain products includes single frames in motion pictures to trigger a craving for a product, like a soft drink, or changing a particular behaviour, such as the feeling of thirst. Albeit the test results vary with regard to the efficiencies of these methods, it is unclear whether this is due to the implementation of the empirical tests or the actual performance of mental processes in the unconscious. Only through ensuring standardised definitions of the mental processes and the measurement criteria will one be able to precisely assess their functions and response to stimuli.[37]

The scientific community now believes the unconscious plays an active part in certain decision-making processes, which is a marked shift from Freud's image of the unconscious as a dustbin of repressed material. And the most current theories on the processes of the unconscious have a distinct advantage over Freud's; they are more data driven, and they lend themselves to clinical testing and empirical validation.

If certain decision-making processes take place outside the conscious, and some seem even not consciously intended, how they are accomplished remains an open question. Psychologists are also interested in how personal judgment and social behaviour operate outside awareness and conscious intent. Similar questions have been addressed on research projects conducted in the area of evolutionary biology and neuroscience. Currently there is agreement among the various sciences that a distinction can be made between unconscious processes and the unconscious mind.

Cognitive research shows the unconscious to be part of an automatic process that registers and stores more information than experienced through the conscious. This appears to happen unintentionally, regardless of conscious goals and instructions. It seems to be a fully automatic unconscious process that is innate in all humans whatever their age, intelligence, culture, education, or other personal factors.[38]

While the unconscious acts as an independent agent outside the control of awareness, it also serves as a complementary partner to the conscious, manifesting itself usually in the form of intuition, gut feelings, eureka moments, déjà vu, and other insights that we are not able to explain rationally.[39]

Conclusion

Although reflections on psychological concepts are probably as old as mankind, some key definitions of concepts such as the mind, consciousness, and free will still remain fluid and difficult to pin down. However, there is now a general consensus that the mind consists of a conscious and an unconscious. Although Sigmund Freud's representation of the mind is now considered obsolete, the concept of the unconscious, albeit in a differing definition, is a recognised part of the mind, as are the various defense mechanisms that exist to handle unpleasant emotions and experiences. These play, as we will see in upcoming chapters, an important part in the sentiments that drive financial bubbles.

Notes

1. Cyber Museum of Neurosurgery, www.neurosurgery.org (accessed November 30, 2013).
2. The Internet Classics Archive, http://classics.mit.edu/Aristotle/soul.html (accessed November 30, 2013).
3. *Online Etymology Dictionary*, 2001, www.etymonline.com (accessed November 30, 2013).
4. Richard Webster, *Why Freud Was Wrong: Sin, Science and Psychoanalysis* (Oxford: The Orwell Press, 2005), 461.
5. Tom Butler-Bowdon, *50 Psychology Classics* (London: Nicholas Brealey Publishing, 2007).
6. American Psychological Association, www.apa.org (accessed November 30, 2013).
7. Saundra K. Ciccarelli and J. Noland White, *Psychology*, 3rd ed. (Upper Saddle River, NJ: Pearson Prentice Hall, 2012).
8. *The American Heritage Dictionary of the English Language*. http://ahdictionary.com/ (accessed November 30, 2013).
9. J. J. C. Smart, "The Mind/Brain Identity Theory," *The Stanford Encyclopedia of Philosophy*, ed. Edward N. Zalta (Fall 2011 Edition), http://plato.stanford.edu/ (accessed November 30, 2013).
10. J. Kim, "Problems in the Philosophy of Mind," in *Problems in the Philosophy of Mind: Oxford Companion to Philosophy*, ed. Ted Honderich (Oxford: Oxford University Press, 1995).
11. Computational Neuroscience Research Group. Waterloo Centre for Theoretical Neuroscience, http://compneuro.uwaterloo.ca/index.html (accessed November 30, 2013).
12. *The Macmillan Dictionary of Psychology*, www.macmillandictionary.com/thesaurus-category/british/Psychology-and-psychoanalysis (accessed November 30, 2013).
13. Max Velmans, "How to Define Consciousness—and How Not to Define Consciousness," *Journal of Consciousness Studies* 16 (2009): 139–156.

14. Hal Blumenfeld, "The Neurological Examination of Consciousness," in *The Neurology of Consciousness: Cognitive Neuroscience and Neuropathology*, ed. Steven Laureys and Giulio Tononi (London: Academic Press, 2009).
15. Rodolfo Llinás, *I of the Vortex: From Neurons to Self* (Cambridge: MA, MIT Press, 2002).
16. Colin Allen, "Animal Consciousness," in *Stanford Encyclopedia of Philosophy*, ed. Edward N. Zalta (Summer 2011 Edition), http://plato.stanford.edu/ (accessed November 30, 2013).
17. Graham Oppy and David Dowe, "The Turing Test," in *Stanford Encyclopedia of Philosophy*, http://plato.stanford.edu/ (accessed November 30, 2013).
18. Abraham H. Maslow, "Instinct Theory Reexamined," in *Motivation and Personality* (New York: Harper & Row, 1954).
19. F. B. Mandal, *Textbook of Animal Behaviour* (Delhi: PHI Learning, 2010).
20. *Merck Manual of Diagnosis and Therapy Home Edition*, "Physical Examination," 06–077c, www.merckmanuals.com (accessed November 30, 2013).
21. *Merriam-Webster Dictionary*, "Instinct," www.merriam-webster.com/ (accessed November 30, 2013).
22. *Encyclopædia Britannica*, "Soul," www.britannica.com/ (accessed November 30, 2013).
23. "Free Will," in *The Stanford Encyclopedia of Philosophy*, ed. Edward N. Zalta (Summer 2011 Edition), http://plato.stanford.edu/ (accessed November 30, 2013).
24. G. Strawson, "Free Will," in *Routledge Encyclopedia of Philosophy*, ed. E. Craig (London: Routledge, 1998, 2004).
25. *Merriam-Webster Dictionary*, www.merriam-webster.com/ (accessed November 30, 2013).
26. Henri F. Ellenberger, *The Discovery of the Unconscious: The History and Evolution of Dynamic Psychiatry* (New York: Basic Books, 1970).
27. Noel Sheehy and Alexandra Forsythe, "Sigmund Freud," in *Fifty Key Thinkers in Psychology* (London: Routledge, 2013).
28. Sigmund Freud, *Group Psychology and the Analysis of the Ego* (New York: Bantam Books, 1960).
29. Heinrich Heine, *The Harz Journey and Selected Prose* (New York: Penguin Classics, 2007).
30. Sigmund Freud, "Beyond the Pleasure Principle" in *On Metapsychology* (Penguin: Middlesex, 1987).
31. Sigmund Freud, *The Unconscious* (London: Penguin Modern Classics Translated Texts, 2005).
32. Ruth Snowden, *Teach Yourself Freud* (New York: McGraw-Hill, 2006), 105–107.
33. Sigmund Freud, *The Ego and the Id* (New York: W. W. Norton & Company, 1990).
34. Anna Freud, *The Ego and the Mechanisms of Defense* (London: Karnac Books, 1992).

35. Ap Dijksterhuis, Pamela K. Smith, Ricjk B. van Baaren, Daniel H. J. Wigboldus, John A. Bargh, and Ezequiel Morsella, "The Unconscious Mind," *Perspectives on Psychological Science* 3, no. 1 (2008): 73–79.
36. Ibid.
37. L. M. Augusto, "Unconscious Knowledge: A Survey," *Advances in Cognitive Psychology* 6 (2010): 116–141.
38. Dan J. Stein, *Cognitive Science and the Unconscious* (Arlington, VA: American Psychiatric Publishing, 1997).
39. Carlin Flora, "Gut Almighty," *Psychology Today* 40, no. 3 (2007): 68–75, and *Oxford English Dictionary*, "Intuition," www.oed.com (accessed November 30, 2013).

References

Allen, Colin. 2011 (Summer). "Animal Consciousness." In *The Stanford Encyclopedia of Philosophy*, edited by Edward N. Zalta.

American Psychological Association, www.apa.org.

The American Heritage Dictionary of the English Language, http://ahdictionary.com/

Augusto, L. M. (2010). "Unconscious Knowledge: A Survey." *Advances in Cognitive Psychology* 6: 116–141.

Blumenfeld, Hal. 2009. "The Neurological Examination of Consciousness." In *The Neurology of Consciousness: Cognitive Neuroscience and Neuropathology*, edited by Steven Laureys and Giulio Tononi. London: Academic Press.

Butler-Bowdon, Tom. 2007. *50 Psychology Classics*. London: Nicholas Brealey Publishing.

Ciccarelli, Saundra K., and J. Noland White. 2012. *Psychology*. 3rd ed. Upper Saddle River, NJ: Pearson Prentice Hall.

Computational Neuroscience Research Group. Waterloo Centre for Theoretical Neuroscience. http://compneuro.uwaterloo.ca/index.html.

Cyber Museum of Neurosurgery, www.neurosurgery.org.

Dijksterhuis, Ap, Pamela K. Smith, Ricjk B. van Baaren, Daniel H. J. Wigboldus, John A. Bargh, and Ezequiel Morsella. 2008. "The Unconscious Mind." *Perspectives on Psychological Science* (January).

Ellenberger, Henri F. 1970. *The Discovery of the Unconscious: The History and Evolution of Dynamic Psychiatry*. New York: Basic Books.

Encyclopedia Britannica. "Soul."

Flora, Carlin. 2007. "Gut Almighty." *Psychology Today* 40(3): 68–75.

"Free Will." 2011 (Summer). In *The Stanford Encyclopedia of Philosophy*, edited by Edward N. Zalta.

Freud, Anna. 1992. *The Ego and the Mechanisms of Defense*. London: Karnac Books.

Freud, Sigmund. 1959. *Group Psychology and the Analysis of the Ego*. New York: Bantam Books.

———. 1990. *The Ego and the Id (The Standard Edition of the Complete Psychological Works of Sigmund Freud)* New York: W. W. Norton & Company.

———. 2005. *The Unconscious*. Penguin Modern Classics Translated Texts.

Heine, Heinrich. 2007. *The Harz Journey and Selected Prose*. Penguin Classics.

The Internet Classics Archive, http://classics.mit.edu/Aristotle/soul.html.

Kim, J. 1995. "Problems in the Philosophy of Mind." In *Oxford Companion to Philosophy*, edited by Ted Honderich. Oxford: Oxford University Press.

Llinás, Rodolfo. 2002. *I of the Vortex: From Neurons to Self*. Cambridge, MA: MIT Press.

The Macmillan Dictionary of Psychology. www.macmillandictionary.com/thesaurus-category/british/Psychology-and-psychoanalysis.

Mandal, F. B. 2010. *Textbook of Animal Behaviour*. Delhi: PHI Learning.

Maslow, Abraham H. 1954. "Instinct Theory Reexamined." In *Motivation and Personality*. New York: Harper & Row.

Merck Manual of Diagnosis and Therapy Home Edition—"Physical Examination." 06-077c. www.merckmanuals.com.

Merriam-Webster Dictionary. "Instinct." www.merriam-webster.com/dictionary/instinct.

———. ———. "Unconscious." www.merriam-webster.com/dictionary/unconscious.

Online Etymology Dictionary. 2001. www.etymonline.com.

Oppy, Graham, and David Dowe. 2011. "The Turing Test. " In *The Stanford Encyclopedia of Philosophy*. http://plato.stanford.edu/.

Oxford English Dictionary. "Intuition." www.oed.com/.

Sheehy, Noel, and Alexandra Forsythe. 2013. "Sigmund Freud." *Fifty Key Thinkers in Psychology*. London: Routledge.

Smart, J. J. C. 2011 (Fall). "The Mind/Brain Identity Theory." In *The Stanford Encyclopedia of Philosophy*, edited by Edward N. Zalta.

Snowden, Ruth. 2006. *Teach Yourself Freud*. New York: McGraw-Hill.

Stein, Dan J. 1997. *Cognitive Science and the Unconscious*. Arlington, VA: American Psychiatric Publishing.

Strawson, G. 1998, 2004. "Free Will." In *Routledge Encyclopedia of Philosophy*, edited by E. Craig. London: Routledge.

Velmans, Max. 2009. "How to Define Consciousness—and How Not to Define Consciousness." *Journal of Consciousness Studies* 16: 139–156.

Webster, Richard. 2005. *Why Freud Was Wrong: Sin, Science and Psychoanalysis*. Oxford: Orwell Press.

CHAPTER 2

Archetypes and Symbols

This chapter provides an overview of Carl Jung's theories of the unconscious, which differed from Freud's theories and which introduce archetypes. Archetypes are innate thought patterns that reside in the unconscious, sharing similarities with instincts and with the proposed power to, under the level of awareness, influence collective behaviour such as trends in the financial markets.

Carl Gustav Jung

The Swiss psychiatrist Carl Gustav Jung (1875–1961) was one of the pioneers of the unconscious and the founding father of analytical psychology (see Figure 2.1). After studying medicine in Basel in 1900, he started work at the renowned Burghölzli Psychiatric Hospital in Zurich. Six years later he contacted Sigmund Freud for the first time, sending him a copy of his book, *The Psychology of Dementia Praecox* (*dementia praecox* is known today as *schizophrenia*). When they met for the first time in Vienna, it was clearly a meeting of minds—they talked for 13 hours—and Freud followed up by sending a collection of his latest essays to the more junior Jung. It was the beginning of a period of close co-operation that lasted until 1913.

Their relationship was a two-way street, particularly as psychology was still in its infancy. Freud played an important role in forming Jung's views, but he also took cues from his younger colleague. Through Freud's book *The Interpretation of Dreams*, Jung became focused on the unconscious, a topic he would spend the rest of his life exploring. Much of his work in those years involved evaluating and empirically applying Freud's psychoanalysis and other treatments on patients at the Burghölzli.

FIGURE 2.1   Carl Gustav Jung

Eventually Jung's research and clinical work caused his views to diverge from those of Freud. In 1912, the divergence became public with the printing of Jung's *Wandlungen und Symbole der Libido* (Psychology of the Unconscious). He had rejected Freud's system of analysing the mind (that is, psychoanalysis) and developed his own system, which he called *analytical psychology*.

Jung regarded Freud's view of the unconscious as incomplete. Whereas Freud viewed it as a dustbin for repressed emotions and desires rejected by the conscious, Jung saw it as composed of two distinct sections—a collective part and an individual part—and believed the unconscious played a more active role in the mind than what Freud proposed. He also dismissed Freud's model of the psyche as arbitrary and too simplistic.[1]

Jung's Theoretical Framework

Jung came to develop his own framework of theories. Some of the important elements include the following:[2]

- The mind's objective is to achieve wholeness by integrating the unconscious into the conscious without compromising its autonomous characteristics, a process Jung called *individuation*. Helping patients achieve individuation is a key part of analytical psychology, the ultimate goal of which is to advance a healthy mental development.
- Elaborating on Freud's psychological anatomy, Jung saw the mind as composed of a conscious and an unconscious, however, with the difference that both parts of the mind also have a personal and a collective part.

- *Synchronicity*—which can be defined as meaningful coincidences between two or more events with no causal connections, thereby reflecting a deeper order that connects the physical and psychological world. For example, you seemingly randomly start to think of someone you have not seen for ages and suddenly the telephone rings and it is that person. This contrasts with *causality*, where for an event to occur, it must be the consequence of a cause. Jung discussed the concept of synchronicity with one of the leading physicists of the time, the Austrian Wolfgang Pauli (1900–1958), in relation to similar phenomena noted in the world of quantum physics. The concept of synchronicity has, however, never been empirically proved and remains highly controversial with many of its critics pointing to confirmation bias in cases of alleged synchronicity.
- The personality tests devised by Jung are the precursors of assessment tests in use today, such as the Myers-Briggs Type Indicator.

The Conscious versus the Unconscious

Jung shared Freud's initial view that the mind is divided into two parts, the conscious and the unconscious, which interact with each other. However, differing from Freud, Jung's research pointed him to additional dimensions of the mind: the personal and the collective.

Whereas the *personal conscious* is unique to each individual, the *collective conscious* is a form of public opinion, a distillation of the average person's cultural and moral values into a set of societal beliefs, norms, attitudes, and mainstream political-isms, such as socialism, liberalism, fascism, or communism, depending on the prevailing context. The values held in the collective conscious tend to be shared among the greater majority of individuals of the group, and with the shared values generally superseding and suppressing any conflicting personal beliefs or values.

The *personal unconscious* is defined by Jung as containing "lost memories, painful ideas that are repressed (i.e., forgotten on purpose), subliminal perceptions, by which are meant sense-perceptions that were not strong enough to reach consciousness, and, finally, contents that are not yet ripe for consciousness."[3] So, like the personal conscious, the contents of the personal unconscious are unique to each individual.

Jung's definition of the personal unconscious comes close to Freud's concept of the unconscious as a whole. But Jung came to believe that something in Freud's model was missing. As his research into schizophrenia progressed, he began questioning the assumption that the human mind develops from a blank slate, a *tabula rasa* at birth. He began to believe that innate, universal patterns existed in the unconscious—separate from the personal unconscious—and that these patterns could influence thought and behaviour. So was born the concept of the *collective unconscious*.

Shared among mankind, the collective unconscious is already present for the newborn. Like instincts or drives, it has a biological base. The universal patterns it contains are a form of genetic memory, the common experiences shared by humanity that have become hard-coded into our DNA over millennia. Jung called these patterns *archetypes*. Figure 2.2 highlights the

FIGURE 2.2   A Graphic Overview of the Relationship between the Personal and Collective, the Conscious and the Unconscious

The figure highlights instincts and DNA as less flexible parts of the interface of the human psychological and physiological set-up.

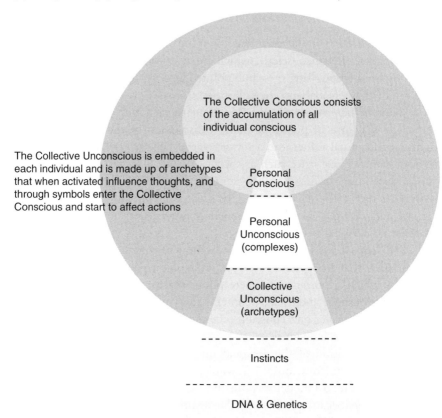

relationship between the personal and collective unconscious and how they embed with the conscious part of the mind and biological instincts.

Archetypes: A Background

Although Freud hinted at concepts similar to archetypes, he never elaborated on them in the way Jung did and it was really after the break-up with Freud that Jung developed his theories on archetypes. It was in his 1919 essay "Instinct and the Unconscious" that Jung introduced and developed the concepts of archetypes. He came to spend much of the rest of his career exploring archetypes, and his views on them never stopped evolving.

Jung developed a number of empirical methods to study the unconscious and in particular archetypes. For example, in his *word association test*, subjects are required to respond quickly when words from a list are read to them, with any delayed responses signalling that unconscious influences are at work. He recorded patients' dreams, fantasies, hallucinations, and visions and searched for patterns and common features. He estimated that he had examined about 67,000 dreams, including his own. He also studied culturally and historically diverse folklore, sagas, myths, and legends in the search for commonalities.

It was through these investigations that Jung identified recurring patterns or themes that seemed to exist collectively regardless of era, culture, or geography—the *archetypes* (from the ancient Greek *arkhetupon*, which can be translated as an original model or die that can be copied).

He believed the archetypes are inherited with the brain structure and hence are biologically encoded. He saw them as being part of man since the earliest days, shaped by evolution and representing the collective history of the human species, the product of the constantly repeated experiences of humanity. So it was apt that Jung referred to them as "the two-million-year-old man that is in us all."[4] Further, and controversially at the time, he posited that the repetitive patterns of the archetypes have brought about physical changes to the brain over the generations. Modern neuroscience has begun to show that he may have been right, but more about that later.

In a 1936 lecture, Jung related archetypes to similar concepts in other academic fields:

> The concept of the archetype, which is an indispensable correlate to the idea of the collective unconscious, indicates the existence of definite forms in the psyche which seem to be present always and everywhere. Mythological

research calls them "motifs"; in the psychology of primitives they correspond to Levy-Bruhl's concept of "representations collectives," and in the field of comparative religion they have been defined by Hubert and Mauss as "categories of the imagination," Adolf Bastian long ago called them "elementary" or "primordial thoughts." From these references, it should be clear enough that my idea of the archetype—literally a pre-existent form—does not stand alone, but is something that is recognised and named in other fields of knowledge.[5]

The Structure of Archetypes

The archetypes share traits with instincts (or the current term *drives*), in being innate from birth and passed on from generation to generation. Whereas instincts are triggers for distinct behaviour—for example, a perception of danger activates the survival instinct, which then triggers the fight or flight response—archetypes regulate perceptions and thought patterns that create *tendencies*, over time, towards altering behaviour, however, with the shared aspiration of ensuring human survival albeit with a longer-term focus.

The archetypes generally lie dormant in the collective unconscious; in other words, they are not actively influencing thoughts and behaviours. But when a catalyst—an event or emotion in conscious reality—creates a sufficiently strong psychological stimulus, an archetype generally somehow related to that catalyst awakes and begins to stimulate the conscious and alter perceptions. *Archetypal images* begin to appear, usually as symbols in visions, dreams, language, and other forms of expression, and eventually affect conscious thinking and prompt a mental context in which differing sets of actions are likely to be taken compared to the pre-archetype era in order to rectify the psychological situation and reduce the likelihood for neurosis.

Because archetypes reside in the unconscious, we are not aware of their existence nor of their influence on our perceptions. As such they are an invisible force, like that of a magnet drawing items in its direction. Even as they become activated, affecting the consciousness and how we grasp reality, they remain obscure. But eventually they are detectable through observing their impact on behaviour and the footprints they leave—the archetypal images. It is through the appearance of archetypal images in the conscious that we are able to infer the existence of the archetypes. The relationship between the archetypes, archetypal images, and symbols is depicted in Figure 2.3.

FIGURE 2.3 An Activated Archetype

An abstract depiction of how an activated archetype transcends into the conscious through the archetypal images and associated symbols. Symbols start to increase in occurrence when an archetype enters consciousness.

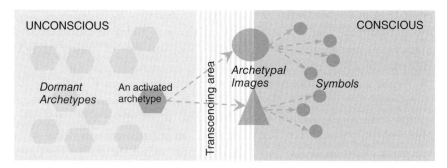

In Jung's words:

Archetypes are irrepresentable in themselves but their effects are discernible in archetypal images and motifs. Archetypes . . . present themselves as ideas and images, like everything else that becomes a content of consciousness.[6]

The way instincts and archetypes affect us can overlap and the boundaries are not always clear cut. However, whereas instincts, in general, are an immediate response to a certain trigger, such as a fight response in the acute danger of a survival situation, an archetype, on the collective level, is a much slower response through the recalibration of thought patterns and over time leads to changes in behaviour.

Archetypes are in form universal regardless of culture; it is their substance that can differ according to the reigning cultural setting and time era. For example, The Warrior is a universal archetype fixed across all cultures, but its substance, how it appears, can change with cultures—the Samurai warrior in Japan, perhaps, the blond Viking in Scandinavia. So the archetypal images need to be studied in the context of the reigning cultural setting in order to understand the archetypal form.

Given that archetypes activate outside of the conscious willpower, how does their autonomous character affect free will? If decision making can take place unconsciously as well as consciously, does this reduce the range of free will? If an activated archetype has the propensity to unconsciously influence your investment strategy to prefer a riskier asset over a risk-free alternative, such as equity over government bonds, are you exercising free will when you indeed choose equities over bonds, albeit possibly rationalising that decision a posteriori?

If it is possible to determine the archetype in force, it should also be possible to understand what the unconscious narrative is, in terms of fixed thought patterns that set constraints on the way reality is perceived and improve the predictive capabilities on the likely outcome of choices, such as allocation of assets, on a collective basis.

While exploring archetypes and their influence on man, Jung was in correspondence with the physicist Wolfgang Pauli. The Nobel laureate commented on the notion of mathematical probabilities and certainties observed in physics. He suggested that archetypes corresponded to a spectrum of probabilities, and that activation would tilt the probabilities towards certain thought patterns supported by the archetype in question, and that could be established through studying their performance in an active state in the past. Jung adopted Pauli's idea and later described the nature of archetypes as:

> It is not . . . a question of inherited ideas but of inherited possibilities of ideas. Nor are they individual acquisitions but, in the main, common to all, as can be seen from [their] universal occurrence.[7]

Jung distinguished between archetypes activated in the collective unconscious with archetypes activated in the personal unconscious, labeling the latter *complexes*. He defined complexes as functional units of the personal unconscious, similar to archetypes being representations of the collective unconscious. However, they differ in that complexes are the bringing together of the general, universal archetypal structures and dispositions with individual memories and experiences and the interpretation of these. A complex will thus take a more individual aspect and will not share the universalities of an archetype. For The Mother archetype, which in the manifestation as a complex in addition to the universal features of motherhood, also would incorporate and strongly emphasise the characteristics and even peculiarities of one's own mother.

A complex can overwrite what is normally perceived as sound judgment and is capable of triggering a distorted reaction towards the feature causing the complex. A key part of Jung's analytical psychology methodology was the treatment of neurosis and other mental disorders stemming from patients' complexes by bring them to the attention of the conscious.[8]

Types of Archetypes

Jung remained ambiguous on the number of archetypes that exist and changed his view throughout his life, even at the very end of his long career; he did say that archetypes are limitless, but he also wrote: "There are as many archetypes as there are typical situations in life."[9] Therefore, an archetype will exist for each universal human experience.

So there is a compelling reason to believe that archetypes are finite, given that they mirror typical human events, ideas, situations, characters, and objects, both human and in nature, which are by definition limited. As a starting point in establishing the number of archetypes, one must ensure that they relate to humanity and its context in a meaningful way. And while Jung never presented an exhaustive list, he did describe a range of archetypes and archetypal categories that are of finite character. It was through his study of patients' dreams and fantasies, as well as his examination of myths and sagas, that Jung defined specific figures, objects, and situations which, irrespective of cultural context or time era, kept recurring and clearly carried significance for the human race. He grouped the archetypes into three categories:

- **Events:** Typical situations in life such as Birth, Death, Rites of Initiation, or Marriage. Within this category one can also include archetypes of transformation, such as Rebirth, and motifs like the Apocalypse.
- **Characters:** Some of these include The Mother, The Father, The Child, God, The Wise Man, The Hero, and The Magician.
- **Objects:** These include natural elements like Water, The Moon, The Sun, Fire, animals like The Snake, The Fish, also Numerals—for example, One is an archetype of order, Two is a contrasting archetype—and also man-made objects, including The Plough or The Sword.[10]

Essentially, the shared characteristic of these archetypes is that they have been part of most, if not all, human communities throughout time. It is important to note that some archetypes, in effect complexes, relate to the individual rather than the collective unconscious. As part of his analytical psychology therapy framework, Jung outlined five main archetypes related to the individual:

1. **The self:** the regulating centre of the mind and facilitator of individuation;
2. **The shadow:** the opposite of the ego, often containing qualities which the ego does not want to identify with or approve of, but which it nonetheless possesses; typically it would consist of negative qualities such as a streak of

sadism or prejudice. This archetype also exists in a collective form, in which it contains aspects of behaviour repressed by society, as a rule projected upon scapegoats;

3. **The anima:** the feminine image in a man's psyche;
4. **The animus:** the masculine image in a woman's psyche; and
5. **The persona:** how we, as individuals, present ourselves to the world. It usually protects the ego from negative images, acting like a mask.[11]

Contradictions become apparent when reviewing Jung's descriptions of archetypes, because he never spelled them out clearly and, to bring order, one needs to clearly align his comments along a timeline to understand when he was doing revisions to previous thinking. Also, his thinking about their make-up changed over time. Adding to the ambiguity, Jung never clearly distinguished or elaborated on the relationship between the underlying archetypes, such as The Sun or The Snake, and their corresponding archetypal images. However, Jungian scholars later reasoned that archetypes would be innately predisposed to producing archetypal images that shared core characteristics, even if they took different forms depending on the prevailing culture and time period. The Sun archetype would produce sun-like archetypal images with key similarities, but they would differ across cultures and era.[12]

Further research into his archetype definitions has seen a number of categories added to those Jung established, in essence not diverting from his original structure but rather further refining it. In particular, the Archive for Research in Archetypal Symbolism (ARAS), a US-based archive focused on the collation of Jungian archetypal imagery has categorised what it considers depictions of symbols with abstract meanings linked to archetypes, though they are not always attaching every specific symbol to individual archetypes.[13] Obviously ARAS's starting point is symbols rather than archetypes. However, by cross-referencing and in parts expanding and elaborating on their symbol categorisation with archetypal categories, as provided by Jung and Jungian disciples, one can attempt to establish a complete and finite set of defined archetypes and map symbols to them that either represent the archetypes or part of their attributes. The ARAS symbol categorisation provides a good start to establish a measurement methodology that tracks archetypal symbols; however, it needs quite a bit of tweaking and calibration to pin and group it to specific archetype clusters rather than individual symbols serving as a measurement base.

The ARAS categories of archetypal symbols are:

- **Creation and Cosmos**
  - Creation and cosmos

- Water
- Air—wind and weather
- Fire—light and darkness
- Earth
- **Plant World**
  - Trees
  - Magical plants
  - Flowers
- **Animal World**
  - Primordial creatures
  - Water creatures
  - Arachnids and insects
  - Birds
  - Wild animals
  - Domestic animals
- **Human World**
  - Human body
  - Movement and expression
  - Fundamentals of work and society
  - Tools and other objects
  - House and home
  - Building and monuments
  - Colour
  - Sound
- **Spirit World**
  - Mythical beings
  - Rituals and sacred systems
  - Sickness and death
  - Soul and psyche

Scientific View of Archetypes

Since Jung's death in 1961, the understanding of the mind has expanded greatly. Among psychologists as well as neuroscientists there is now broad acceptance, although not consensus, of the existence of an unconscious part of the mind, including one with shared collective features. Whether the current view matches Jung's model at an abstract level is still the subject of debate. It is unlikely that we will be able to link specific parts of the brain with specific archetypes. This differs from the more simplistic instincts, such as fear, which can be attributed, at least partly, to specific parts of the brain, given that their nature draws on numerous functions of the brain—perceptual, emotional, motivational, attentional, memory, and so on. Being dynamic, as well as having active and dormant states, makes it difficult to connect archetypes to distinct parts or processes of the brain, at least given the current status of the understanding of the brain.

As Jung pointed out in 1936, concepts similar to archetypes appear in other academic disciplines and that list has since further expanded. And although there never have been attempts to formally connect them in a multidisciplinary approach, archetypes do seem to share a number of characteristics. They are:

- Innate in nature and part of the human psychological make-up;
- Universal and recur throughout humankind's cultural evolution over time;
- Finite in number; and
- Generally different from instincts in terms of being less constrained in their direct manifestations in response to catalysts.

In his book, *Archetypes: A Natural History of the Self*, Anthony Stevens lists several notions that are similar to the characteristics of archetypes:

- In mythology there is the concept of *motifs*.
- The French philosopher Lucien Lévy-Bruhl (1857–1939) referred to *représentations collectives* in the psychology of primitives.
- In comparative religion, terms such as *categories of imagination* and *primordial thoughts* are being used. Some psychology disciplines talk about *isomorphs* and *behavioural systems.*
- Anthropology has *biogrammar*, and the American philosopher Noam Chomsky established the concepts of *language acquisition device* and *deep structure* in psycholinguistics, theorising that all languages share a common root grammar, adjusted to fit the brain's capability to handle signals and abstractions.
- The French anthropologist Claude Lévi-Strauss (1908–2009) referred to a hidden order in the infrastructure of the mind that enables humans, regardless of cultural context or geography, to establish and maintain society and customs in similar ways.
- The ethologists and Nobel laureates Konrad Lorenz (1903–1989) and Niko Tinbergen (1907–1988) developed the concept of *innate releasing mechanisms*, pointing to preprogrammed behaviour that can be triggered by specific signals, independent of learning.[14]

In sociobiology, it is assumed that our social behaviour has developed through evolution, is inherited, and is affected by natural selection through the generations in the same way natural selection moulds physical and biological features. That behaviour is written into and embedded in the DNA. Sociobiologists and others now believe that humans (and animals) repeat acts that have proved advantageous from an evolutionary point of view. Therefore, it is possible in certain situations—those relating to evolutionary adaptation and survival—to forecast individual and collective human behaviour.[15]

A more controversial concept is that of *morphic fields*, introduced by the English biochemist and parapsychologist Rupert Sheldrake. His thesis is that morphic fields exist within and around morphic units—which can be seen as repetitions of similar acts or thoughts. These fields will then organise their structure and activity patterns around the particular morphic unit. Sheldrake views these morphic fields as a sort of all-encompassing repository of acts or thoughts shared by mankind and passed on over generations. Although Sheldrake's concept has not won much support in the scientific community and remains unproved, it provides yet another example of shared similarities with the Jungian concept of archetypes.[16]

More indirect support for Jung's archetypal proposition comes from *epigenetics*, the study of how individual genes can be activated or deactivated through life experiences and/or the environment. It has been shown that the effects of behaviour or events in one lifetime can be genetically passed on to the next generation, causing a sudden "evolutionary" change. Rather than changing the DNA structure, a specific behaviour or event switches on or off particular genes in the DNA, and those genes remain switched on or off in the DNA passed on to the next coming generation, with the capacity to affect both the offsprings' mental and physical health. The study of geographical regions with starvation or other severe environmental conditions has shown that these conditions can cause a change in genes that may be passed on within one generation, something quite contrary to previous perceptions that evolutionary changes take place over hundreds of generations or longer.[17]

In his 2012 book, *The Neurobiology of the Gods*, Erik D. Goodwyn examines the most up-to-date evolutionary and cognitive neuroscientific research on archetypes, seeking a way to understand them in terms of brain physiology.[18] He documents extensive research that points to a neuroscientific basis for archetypal patterns. However, others, such as Christian Roesler in an article in the *Journal of Analytical Psychology,* "Are Archetypes Transmitted

More by Culture Than Biology?" argue that epigenetics in fact raises questions about many of Jung's basic assumptions.[19] New findings in neuroscience provide more and more insight into the functions of the brain and links to the hitherto abstract notion of the mind. While this area of study is still considered a frontier science, whose foundations are far from stabilised, the thinking changes constantly as new findings are published and seems to be moving closer to supporting evidence of brain features that in functionality come very close to archetypes in the way that Jung fathomed them.

So today there is an extended consent that a collective unconscious and associated thought patterns exist, however one choses to label them. There is also broad scientific agreement that we have a kind of genetic memory, a tendency hard-coded into our DNA to respond in certain ways to certain stimuli. The notion that at birth our mind is a blank slate, a *tabula rasa*, has been discarded and proven erroneous.

The concept of archetypes, though described in different ways, is accepted in a variety of academic disciplines to explain seemingly hard-coded human behavioural patterns and the triggers that release them. However, there is still much discussion and disagreement on their exact nature, function, and ability to influence behaviour.

Why Do Archetypes Activate?

While Carl Jung and his disciples have provided some rationale on why archetypes can seem to suddenly activate from a dormant state, a raft of questions remains on the functions of the catalysts. We do, however, know that archetypes are autonomous and intentional, meaning that they do not activate randomly but with a purpose to act in *certain ways* in *certain situations* to achieve *certain objectives* that we are not aware of consciously and therefore cannot actively impact.

Compensating for a Single-Sided Conscious Attitude

One of the central functions of the unconscious is to act as a compensating force to a conscious attitude that has become too single sided. In other words, an archetype activates when the collective conscious has deviated too far from the sentiments required to maintain mental stability. This may be observed in a society pushed into imbalance through exhausting itself by extrapolating the momentum of the reigning zeitgeist into its extreme—or from the perspective of finance, the euphoric culmination of a price bubble. This fact is generally clearly recognised only in hindsight through the excesses that at another time take absurd appearances.

It is this psychological imbalance that acts as the catalyst that triggers the activation of an archetype with the objective to start to weaken and eventually replace the "unhealthy" conscious attitudes. As the overarching aspiration of the mind is to help rectify the imbalance that the one-sided conscious is causing, an archetype will, over time, through its activation either prompt a counteraction or a complementary collective behaviour through entering the conscious. Once psychological equilibrium has been achieved through the archetype-induced, changed thought pattern, the activated archetype's energy will eventually succumb in the conscious part of the mind, replacing the old conscious perception of reality with a new one and the archetype itself, thus having fulfilled the objective of the mind, will then recede back into slumber. If this newly formed conscious attitude over time leads to excesses with the risk of pushing the mental equilibrium out of tilt, the process is repeated and another archetype will activate to restore balance.

How are these imbalanced conscious attitudes triggered in the first place? It is through the emergence of psychological repressions in a society where certain attitudes and desires have come to be considered unacceptable by reigning conventions and norms, and even sometimes by decree, and therefore these notions have to be subdued and self-censored and cannot enter the public arena and be openly discussed. The Victorian era of censuring and suppressing even remote references to anything of a sexual nature is an atypical example of an unbalanced collective conscious that has been allowed to dominate a society. The various defense mechanisms are applied to handle the forbidden thoughts but if the amount of repressed material becomes overwhelming, there is a risk that the conscious attitude becomes too narrow-minded, from the mind's holistic perspective, and can give rise to various forms of neurotic behaviour and social anxieties. These anxieties can include anything from moral panics, witch hunts, and various types of aggressive activities, and in extreme cases, even violence on a massive scale, which the zealous acceptance and commitment to political-isms and dogmas have highlighted.

Compensating for Capacity Issues in the Conscious Part of the Mind

Psychological imbalances can also appear through the forced selection and focus of the conscious towards certain attitudes and norms on the simple grounds that the conscious part of the mind can handle only so many differing sentiments at a time. This need to exclude perspectives, due to capacity issues, will also lead to the sorting out of attitudes deemed less relevant or irrelevant, not necessarily considered politically incorrect but unapt in the existing context, and hence will not be allowed to enter the conscious. Again, like keeping back certain impulses, this selection will create a tendency towards single-sided orientations in the conscious mind and can, if deemed unhealthy from the broader perspective, give rise to the activation of archetypes in order to restore a psychological balance. However, differing from the less permissive society which forbids certain attitudes, a society where capacity issues can arise, possible through the parallel existence of a plethora of opinions and perspectives, is not as strained in adjusting its societal psychological status and therefore the necessity of activating an archetype becomes less likely.

Providing Assistance to a Conscious Not Sufficiently Equipped to Resolve an Emerging and Particular Situation

When a psychological situation suddenly occurs which the prevailing conscious attitude is not equipped to resolve, an archetype with a thought pattern deemed suitable activates and pushes into the conscious to facilitate the mental support to address the situation. The type of situation is not restricted to different forms of crises suddenly arising and causing psychological disturbances but could also include terms of extended euphoria that need to be toned down to restore equilibrium. Examples include paradigm shifts due to exogenous factors or new innovations that in some way drastically change the way reality needs to be perceived, rendering existing psychical notions less suitable, and thus to be able to cope with reality, activations of archetypes deemed more suitable are initiated. Jung pointed out that a particular archetype, The Wise Man, could activate when the human collective is out of synch and likely to go astray from a psychological perspective; this typically could happen around greater paradigm shifts, whether technical, political, or other.[20]

Release of Psychic Energy

The activation of archetypes releases psychic energy, or libido, which enables the advance of archetypal thought patterns and behaviours into the conscious. Jung assigned the libido a broader definition than Freud's, which he first saw as exclusively being a sexual energy and later driven by the pleasure and reality principles. Jung, however, perceived libido as being a more general and creative psychic energy.[21]

How does psychic energy perform in the activation process?

First of all, the approach to track and understand the archetypal activity is done through gauging its energy levels, which will differ from a dormant state where they do not impact and motivate to various levels of energetic states when they start to influence through triggering patterns of thought structures. Once one can assess each archetype's energy level, it is possible to make forecasts on whether a specific archetype has activated and started to engage the general collective.

Jung argued that psychic energy will leave traces in forms of symbols that will appear in various milieus. Subsequently, if one is able to measure the occurrence and frequency of these symbols, as acting proxies for psychic energies, one could then infer the levels of the archetypal transformation in the mind.

Jung shared the view with Freud that psychic energy would follow the same laws as physical energy; therefore, psychic energy can neither be created nor destroyed, it will just change from one state to another. In other words, when an unconscious archetype starts to increase energy levels, an equivalent amount of decreasing energy would have to occur somewhere else in the mind. He applied the principle of entropy, suggesting that in a sealed energy system, differences in energy intensities eventually would even out and stabilise each other, striving towards an equilibrium.[22]

Although neither Freud nor Jung was able to scientifically prove the existence of psychic energy, currently there exists extensive research and documentation pointing out that mental effort and activity do correspond to metabolic increases in the brain's neurons. Neuroscientists have been able to measure and estimate these movements through fMRI (functional magnetic resonance imaging) scans.[23]

Transcending Function

Jung labeled the mind's aspiration towards a psychological equilibrium to ensure long-term survival, *individuation*. According to Jung, individuation is achieved through the integration of the unconscious with the conscious.[24]

Individuation takes places both on an individual and a collective level; however, the urge for individuation for the collective overrides that of the specific individual and if conflicting in psychological direction can lead to neurotic behaviour for the individual.

As archetypal images start to transcend into the conscious as part of individuation to ensure the fulfillment of equilibrium, it is facilitated by a *transcending function* that will ease the interaction of the archetypal force into the conscious. This transcending function arises from the energy tension between consciousness and the unconscious and supports their union. It is labeled "transcendent" as it makes the transition from one attitude sentiment to another organically possible. The transcendent function forms part of the self-regulation of the mind, together with individuation.[25]

Seemingly Spontaneous Activation

In essence, the activation of archetypes will trigger from three catalysts:

1. When certain attitudes and norms become constrained by the conscious and a risk of imbalances in the mind exists that can eventually result in neurotic behaviour;
2. As a compensation to rebalance capacity issues in the conscious part of the mind; and
3. When the present conscious attitudes are not equipped to handle an emerging changing reality or psychological circumstance.

However, as it is generally not obvious for a community or society at large that its attitudes and norms have become skewed in a way that might lead to neurosis and social illnesses, given that they are caught up and formed by the reigning zeitgeist, the activation of archetypes to address psychological deficiencies might appear spontaneous once they have entered awareness and their physical manifestations can be observed, albeit generally only in hindsight. This makes it difficult to forecast which archetypes will arise and when they will activate.

It is important to note that it is not true that the unconscious attitudes will always contrast with the dominant conscious mindset but that they can also take a more complementary form. The appearance of the corresponding archetypes' symbolic manifestations will indicate their character and content. Thus, one cannot automatically project an opposing polarised psychological reaction to an existing mentally imbalanced environment.

Jung stated that when the mind starts working on restoring equilibrium through activating the archetype, the outlet of the archetypal activation itself is likely to lead to behaviours with *pathological* characteristics.[26] This would include various types of neurotic and erratic behaviours that when appearing in societal situations could, depending on the magnitude of the force of the archetypal energy, span from obsessions to noticeably bizarre and odd fads and trends that suddenly seem to appear from nowhere, to the abrupt flare-up of civil unrest, demonstrations, riots, revolutions, and even war.

Regardless of the rationale for archetypes to activate, it is important to note that the process is essentially a transformation, in which archetypes are activated and brought into the conscious and assimilated into the collective conscious disposition. This means that from activation in the unconscious until the embedding into the collective conscious, the archetypes will exert an influence on human actions and behaviours.

An additionally important characteristic is that archetypes are neither a negative nor a positive force. The activation of an archetype with aggressive characteristics need not necessarily be viewed as negative but can be triggered as a psychological force to restore a society dominated by apathetic attitudes and lethargy, although the consequences of such an archetype activating might well lead to increased violent displays in society. As the archetype is a dynamic, autonomous agent that directs our actions in ways of which we initially are not aware of or can consciously control, it becomes, on a collective basis, difficult to break or diverge its influence once it has activated.

Symbols: The Tangible Manifestations of Archetypes

Jung pointed out that one of the central functions of the unconscious was that of symbol creating.[27] As archetypes reside in the unconscious, it is not possible to directly observe them, but through the archetypal images and by pinning down the related symbols to each specific archetype, one can develop a taxonomy that can be used as a tracking mechanism to gauge archetypal energy levels and impacts. So once specific archetypes activate, they start to leave traces in the form of symbols which can be observed and gathered from a variety of outlets.

A *symbol* is defined as something that represents an idea, a process, or a physical entity. The word itself derives from the ancient Greek *symbolon*, meaning "token" or "watchword." Symbols come in many forms, images being the most obvious representation; however, there are also word symbols as well as symbolic rituals and activities, predominantly religious ones.[28] The use of symbols seems to be an exclusively human form of communication and goes back to the first days of humankind, with the earliest identified symbols found in caves in Europe and dating to 30,000 years ago. Given that symbols impact most, if not all, aspects of human behaviour, reviews of symbols are generally included in academic disciplines such as psychology, culture, religion, art, architecture, and literature.[29]

It is, however, important to distinguish between symbols and signs. Both symbols and signs aim at conveying meaning; where they differ is in terms of abstraction. A sign stands for something known; for example, a stop sign means stop and nothing else. Thus the meaning of a sign is absolutely known, resting on conventions or collectively made conscious agreements.[30]

In contrast, a symbol, in addition to its apparent superficial meaning, also holds an abstract meaning, which usually has little to do with the dictionary explanation of the symbol itself. It is this abstract meaning that links to the unconscious. To the conscious, this aspect of the symbol is not picked up on as it represents an archetypal thought structure coming to the forefront. So, by observing an increased use of such symbol words, when and only when they represent the specific archetypal images and through that linked to the archetypes themselves, one can start to understand what type of specific thought patterns and perceptions are being influenced by the unconscious and draw inferences to what sort of collective behaviour might result. Symbols, therefore, provide a unique feature in that they directly access the unconscious on an otherwise not approachable path through conscious means. Through extensive testing and research in analytical psychology, it is generally agreed that people do absorb and relate to archetypal symbols at the unconscious level.[31]

Jung considered symbols to be energy and information carriers that hold, incorporate, and transform psychological energy. The same energy that activates the archetypes, and through the individuation process and transcending function, embeds them into the conscious part of the mind as a new psychological equilibrium. Jung was clear that it was through the analysis and understanding of symbols that archetypes can be understood.

He made a point of differentiating between natural symbols and cultural symbols, where natural symbols represent the archaic and elementary roots stemming from his two-million-year-old man concept and the repeated experiences of humanity's common characteristics. The cultural symbols, however, express "the eternal truths" and are often connected to the religious or esoteric sphere.[32]

Symbols as Expressions

The attributes of the various archetypes are represented by their equivalent symbols; for example, aggressive or war-related archetypes are featured in the appearance of war-like symbols, expressed both as words and depictions, occurring in non-war-like contexts used as figurative language. As a specific archetype activates, the corresponding symbols suddenly come into fashion and are used with increased frequency, unknowingly by the users, who do not detect or understand that an unconscious force is starting to influence their thought patterns. Eventually wider and wider groups of people start to use these symbols to describe various aspects of everyday life and surroundings and consequently they spread and become fashionable and increasingly used; in time, the archetypal perception changes the way reality is being experienced for the broader collective.

Now, given that archetypes are reflected through the abstract meanings of symbol words rather than their literal meaning, it requires that one only review accounts when words are used in figurative language, whether as euphemisms, proverbs, metaphors, or similar literary devices applied for description. So the crafting of a concise and all-encompassing dictionary of symbols requires translating the abstract meaning of symbols and connecting them to the archetypes they represent in order to decode archetypal activities, ensuring that these symbols are being picked up by an appropriate methodology.

The relationship between symbols and their influence on behaviour has been studied both from the individual perspective and the collective, especially when applied in advertising. Advertisers and researchers of consumer patterns have long deployed symbols that implicitly or unconsciously relate to motherly comfort, strength and reliability, prestige, sexual appeal, or other typically positive attributes they want their product associated with. In individual patient cases, with behaviour considered abnormal or neurotic, it has been demonstrated that such behaviour can be triggered or accentuated through exposure to symbols representing the root of the mental ailments. For example, if someone has suppressed the memories of being abused as a child by a person regularly dressed in red clothing, in adult life, just the sight of the colour red can trigger anxiety in that person due to the symbolic meaning of pain and abuse that red has come to represent to him or her. As part of the treatment, it becomes one of the psychoanalyst's main tasks to identify the symbolic meaning of the triggers that release neurosis.

However, there seems to be no single generally accepted approach on how to identify symbols that can be understood by their culturally transmitted meanings and how to link them to archetypes. This fact has been noted within the research community and the ARAS (Archive for Research in Archetypal Symbolism) categorisation of archetypal images to which one can attach related symbols and which serves as the most comprehensive dictionary of symbols in place. The ARAS symbol dictionary can be applied as an initial straw man that with some significant adjustments can be developed to form the base structure of a symbol measurement model.[33]

Symbols as Archetypal Proxies

Whether something should be interpreted as a symbol or a sign ultimately depends on the predominant attitude of society. Some symbols become widely used in a given societal context; those symbols and their abstract meanings often become so culturally pervasive that they evolve into a lasting part of both the culture and the way the culture conveys itself. For example, the symbol *lion* in many cultures holds the abstract representation of courage; the *heart* most often symbolises love; and the *dragon* symbol in Chinese culture generally stands for majesty and power, whereas in Western culture it tends to symbolises evil. So the associating of archetypal images to symbols requires a correct interpretation of the prevailing cultural context. However, if the symbolic meaning transcends and in effect replaces the word's literal meaning and can be fully explained in a way we perceive as entirely rational, or its abstract charge loses its power and becomes unknown, then the symbol relapses into a sign. There is also the case where the archetypal charge of a symbol over time has decayed and eventually expired and becomes part of an acknowledged conventional meaning and therefore it turns into a "dead" symbol. Examples of dead symbols are the various symbolic terms that used to represent the ancient mythology of Greek and Roman gods, and most of this vocabulary would now fail to resonate in any manner. The abstract meaning of a true symbol can never be fully consciously comprehended as the use of figurative languages in the coming chapters will highlight; however, it can be broadly understood and interpreted out of context.

The meaning of an archetypal symbol gets determined through collective experience and cultural phenomena, in the same way that archetypal contents get formed over time. Furthermore, the mental processes of individuals communicating, whether consciously or unconsciously, are often encoded into the transmission and interpretation of the specific symbols. Freudians see symbols being used as part of the *displacement* defense mechanism where the symbols serve as the "safe" objects to which the mind redirects from the "unsafe" objects.

Establishing whether symbols contain an archetypal meaning will therefore hinge upon whether they contain, in addition to their literal meaning, an abstract meaning in their commonly applied usage.

Jungian analytics rests on the assumption that through reversing the direction and following the symbols, one can access the archetype and apprehend when a particular symbol gains importance through increased usage. It will also reflect the surrounding circumstances when the corresponding archetype has activated and can then be analysed to better understand the catalysts.[34]

The symbol's energy intensity can therefore be measured through gauging its frequency from a suite of publications and other media outlets with a wide

FIGURE 2.4 Abstract Depiction of Symbols as Energy, an Information Carrier between the Unconscious and the Conscious

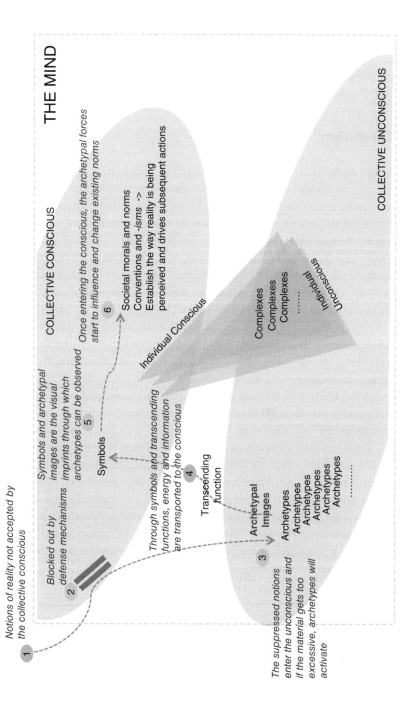

49

enough coverage and circulation to reverberate with the general perceptions and sentiments, and as the underlying archetypal activities fluctuate, this will be reflected in the occurrences of the corresponding symbols. Figure 2.4 provides a graphical overview of how symbols operate as carriers of information and energy between the unconscious and the conscious.

Conclusion

Jung's archetypes share many key features with concepts in other academic disciplines, albeit labelled differently. Since the term *archetype* was coined, it was never really written off by contemporary science; in fact, the current stance of neuroscience comes close, if not conclusive, to pointing to the existence of processes in the brain similar to the proposed Jungian archetypes. The existence of such innate mental structures with the possibility to measure them would provide a unique opportunity to understand when a new thought pattern is about to activate, and then make estimates on the likely behviour it might lead to in society at large or investment patterns.

Archetypes do not activate randomly from the holistic perspective of the mind; instead, they are part of a mental mechanism to ensure the long-term well-being of the collective mind, not unlike the triggering of instincts to ensure mankind's survival. If equipped with the understanding of when an archetype is likely to activate and change perceptions and behaviour, one can start to look for its tangible manifestations, namely symbols, to understand its characteristics and directions.

Jung saw the creation of symbols as one of the key functions of the unconscious, because such symbols will carry an additional meaning to that of a sign. This figurative, rather than literal, meaning of a symbol is what conveys the unconscious influence on perceptions and an increasing trend of a certain theme of symbols, such as war-like ones that can indicate a change towards more aggressive behaviour. Thus, if one is able to capture the occurrence of symbols on a comprehensive basis, reflecting the broader sentiment in society, this would serve as a proxy to measure archetypal activity.

Notes

1. Clare Dunne, *Carl Jung: Wounded Healer of the Soul: An Illustrated Biography* (London: Continuum International Publishing Group, 2002).
2. Ibid.

3. C. G. Jung, *The Archetypes and the Collective Unconscious* (Vol. 9, Part 1 of *The Collected Works of C. G. Jung*), trans. R. F. C. Hull, 2nd ed. (Princeton, NJ: Princeton University Press, 1981), par. 103.

4. Anthony Stevens and David H. Rosen, *The Two Million-Year-Old Self* (Carolyn and Ernest Fay Series in Analytical Psychology) (College Station, TX: Texas A&M University Press, 2005).

5. Jung, *The Archetypes and the Collective Unconscious*, 87–110.

6. C. G. Jung, *Concerning the Archetypes and the Anima Concept* (Vol. 9, Part 1 of *The Collected Works of C. G. Jung*), trans. R. F. C. Hull, 2nd ed. (Princeton, NJ: Princeton University Press, 1981), par. 136.

7. C. G. Jung, *On the Nature of the Psyche* (Vol. 8 of *The Collected Works of C. G. Jung*), trans. R. F. C. Hull, 2nd ed. (Princeton, NJ: Princeton University Press, 1981), par. 435.

8. C. G. Jung, *Psychotherapy and a Philosophy of Life* (Vol. 16 of *The Collected Works of C. G. Jung*), trans. R. F. C. Hull, 2nd ed. (Princeton, NJ: Princeton University Press, 1981), par. 179.

9. Calvin S. Hall and Vernon J. Nordby, *A Primer of Jungian Psychology* (New York: Plume, 1999).

10. Anthony Stevens, "The Archetypes," Chapter 3 in *The Handbook of Jungian Psychology: Theory, Practice and Applications*, ed. Renos K. Papadopoulos (New York: Routledge, 2006).

11. Murray Stein, *Jung's Map of the Soul: An Introduction* (Chicago: Open Court, 1998), 106.

12. C. G. Jung, *Man and His Symbols* (New York: Dell, 1968).

13. The Archive for Research in Archetypal Symbolism, *The Book of Symbols: Reflections on Archetypal Images* (Cologne, Germany: Taschen, 2010).

14. Anthony Stevens, *Archetype Revisited: An Updated Natural History of the Self* (Studies in Jungian Psychology by Jungian Analysts), 2nd sub ed. (Toronto: Inner City Books, 2003).

15. Edward O. Wilson, *Sociobiology: The New Synthesis, Twenty-Fifth Anniversary Edition* (Cambridge, MA: Belknap Press of Harvard University Press, 2000).

16. Tim Adams, "Rupert Sheldrake: The 'Heretic' at Odds with Scientific Dogma," *The Guardian*, February 4, 2012; Rupert Sheldrake, *Morphic Resonance: The Nature of Formative Causation* (South Paris, ME: Park Street Press, 2009).

17. Richard C. Francis, *Epigenetics: How Environment Shapes Our Genes* (New York: W. W. Norton & Company, 2012).

18. Erik D. Goodwyn, *The Neurobiology of the Gods: How Brain Physiology Shapes the Recurrent Imagery of Myth and Dreams* (New York: Routledge, 2012).

19. Christian Roesler, "Are Archetypes Transmitted More by Culture Than Biology?" *Journal of Analytical Psychology* 57, no. 2 (2012): 223–246.

20. C. G. Jung, *Modern Man in Search of a Soul* (New York: Harcourt Harvest, 1955).

21. C. G. Jung, *On the Nature of the Psyche* (Princeton, NJ: Princeton University Press, 1969).

22. Ibid.

23. D. Parker Benton, P. Y. Parker, and R. T. Donohoe, "The Supply of Glucose to the Brain and Cognitive Functioning," *Journal of Biosocial Science* 28 (1996): 463–479; S. H. Fairclough and K. Houston, "A Metabolic Measure of Mental Effort," *Biological Psychology* 66 (2004): 177–190.

24. Jung, *The Archetypes and the Collective Unconscious*, par. 237.

25. C. G. Jung, *The Transcendent Function* (Vol. 8 in *The Collected Works of C. G. Jung*), trans. R. F. C. Hull, 2nd ed. (Princeton, NJ: Princeton University Press, 1981), par. 145.

26. C. G. Jung, *The Role of the Unconscious* (Vol. 10 in *The Collected Works of C. G. Jung*), trans. R. F. C. Hull, 2nd ed. (Princeton, NJ: Princeton University Press, 1981), 20–26.

27. C. G. Jung, *Civilization in Transition* (Vol. 10 in *The Collected Works of C.G. Jung*), trans. R. F. C. Hull, 2nd ed. (Princeton, NJ: Princeton University Press, 1981), par. 18.

28. Joseph Campbell, *The Flight of the Wild Gander: Explorations in the Mythological Dimension* (New York: HarperPerennial, 1991).

29. Rodger Morrison, "New Method of Identifying Archetypal Symbols and Their Associated Meanings," *European Journal of Social Sciences* 27 (2011).

30. Miranda Bruce Mitford, *Signs and Symbols* (New York: DK Publishing, 2008).

31. Morrison, "New Method of Identifying Archetypal Symbols."

32. C. G. Jung, *Man and His Symbols* (Dell, 1968).

33. Morrison, "New Method of Identifying Archetypal Symbols."

34. C. G. Jung, *C.G. Jung Speaking*, ed. R. F. C. Hull, reprint ed. (Princeton, NJ: Princeton University Press, 1987), 72.

References

The Archive for Research in Archetypal Symbolism. 2010. *The Book of Symbols, Reflections on Archetypal Images*. Cologne, Germany: Taschen.

Adams, Tim. 2012. "Rupert Sheldrake: The 'Heretic' at Odds with Scientific Dogma." *The Guardian*, February 4.

Benton, D., P. Y. Parker, and R. T. Donohoe. 1996. "The Supply of Glucose to the Brain and Cognitive Functioning." *Journal of Biosocial Science* 28(4): 463–479.

Campell, Joseph. 1991. *The Flight of the Wild Gander: Explorations in the Mythological Dimension*. New York: HarperPerennial.

Dunne, Clare. 2002. *Carl Jung: Wounded Healer of the Soul: An Illustrated Biography*. New York: Continuum International Publishing Group.

Francis, Richard C. 2012. *Epigenetics: How Environment Shapes Our Genes*. New York: W. W. Norton & Company.

Goodwyn, Erik D. 2012. *The Neurobiology of the Gods: How Brain Physiology Shapes the Recurrent Imagery of Myth and Dreams*. New York: Routledge.

Hall, Calvin S., and Nordby, Vernon J. 1999. *A Primer of Jungian Psychology*. New York: Plume.

Jung, C. G. 1955. *Modern Man in Search of a Soul*. New York: Harcourt Harvest.

———. 1968. *Man and His Symbols*. New York: Dell.

———. 1969. *On the Nature of the Psyche*. Princeton, NJ: Princeton University Press.

———. 1981. *The Archetypes and the Collective Unconscious*. Vol. 9, Part 1 of *The Collected Works of C. G. Jung*. Translated by R. F. C. Hull. 2nd ed. Princeton, NJ: Princeton University Press.

———. 1981. *Civilization in Transition*. Vol. 10 in *The Collected Works of C. G. Jung*. Translated by R. F. C. Hull. 2nd ed. Princeton, NJ: Princeton University Press.

———. 1981. *Concerning the Archetypes and the Anima Concept*. Vol. 9, Part 1 of *The Collected Works of C. G. Jung*. Translated by R. F. C. Hull. 2nd ed. Princeton, NJ: Princeton University Press.

———. 1981. *On the Nature of the Psyche*. Vol. 8 of *The Collected Works of C. G. Jung*. Translated by R. F. C. Hull. 2nd ed. Princeton, NJ: Princeton University Press.

———. 1981. *Psychotherapy and a Philosophy of Life*. Vol. 16 of *The Collected Works of C. G. Jung*. Translated by R. F. C. Hull. 2nd ed. Princeton, NJ: Princeton University Press.

———. 1981. *The Role of the Unconscious*. Vol. 10 of *The Collected Works of C. G. Jung*. Translated by R. F. C. Hull. 2nd ed. Princeton, NJ: Princeton University Press.

———. 1981. *The Transcendent Function*. Vol. 8 of *The Collected Works of C. G. Jung*. Translated by R. F. C. Hull. 2nd ed. Princeton, NJ: Princeton University Press.

———. 1987. *C. G. Jung Speaking*. Translated by R. F. C. Hull. Reprint edition. Princeton, NJ: Princeton University Press.

Mitford, Miranda Bruce. 2008. *Signs and Symbols*. New York: DK Publishing.

Morrison, Rodger. 2011. "New Method of Identifying Archetypal Symbols and their Associated Meanings." *European Journal of Social Sciences* 27.

Roesler, Christian. 2012. "Are Archetypes Transmitted More by Culture Than Biology?" *Journal of Analytical Psychology* 57(2): 223–246.

Sheldrake, Rupert. 2009. *Morphic Resonance: The Nature of Formative Causation*. South Paris, ME: Park Street Press.

Stein, Murray. 1998. *Jung's Map of the Soul: An Introduction*. Chicago: Open Court.

Stevens, Anthony. 2003. *Archetype Revisited: An Updated Natural History of the Self (Studies in Jungian Psychology by Jungian Analysts)* 2nd ed. Toronto: Inner City Books.

———. 2006. "The Archetypes." In *The Handbook of Jungian Psychology: Theory, Practice and Applications*, edited by Renos K. Papadopoulos, New York: Routledge.

———, and David H. Rosen. 2005. *The Two Million-Year-Old Self (Carolyn and Ernest Fay Series in Analytical Psychology)* College Station, TX: Texas A&M University Press.

Wilson, Edward O. 2000. *Sociobiology: The New Synthesis, Twenty-Fifth Anniversary Edition*. Cambridge, MA: Belknap Press of Harvard University Press.

CHAPTER 3

How Archetypes Influence and Impact Behaviour

When an archetype activates, it can be noted through a number of psychological mechanisms that influence behaviour. These manifestations include the introduction of a new zeitgeist that shines a light on how reality is viewed and what is dimmed out. Anything or anyone that seems to be deviating from it is subject to being projected onto a scapegoat, something which history has shown carries great risk. Panics and hysteria are other neurotic reactions that can arise out of a changing psychological environment. All of these features will be discussed in this chapter.

Characteristics of the Activation of an Archetype

When an archetype has activated and the archetypal force begins influencing thought patterns, the thinking of the human collective tends to bend. This effect is particularly apparent in mass movements and moves in the financial markets. Because the archetypal force influencing behaviour is initiated at the unconscious level, on the conscious level the behaviour will appear to have been spontaneous. The awakening of an archetype produces a compulsion towards certain ideas, and can in itself initially trigger another state of neurosis, in contrast or complementary to the neurotic imbalances it was set to resolve. Before an archetype is embedded in the conscious and a new equilibrium is restored, its entry into the conscious world can take the form of a sort of birth pang.[1]

Carl Jung saw politics as the area where archetypes had their strongest impact, especially in times of crisis, when the associated anxiety could activate archetypes. He proposed that the earliest signs of archetypal involvement would be in the form of psychological disruptions "mostly in the form of abnormal over- or under-valuations which provoke misunderstandings, quarrels, fanaticisms, and follies of every description . . . in this way there grow up modern myth-formations, i.e., fantastic rumours, suspicions, prejudices."[2] It is important to note that the reaction to the awakening of the archetype does not come from outside the collective, but from within, as the behaviour pattern already exists within—and therefore becomes possible to forecast.

As the psychological mood starts changing due to the archetypal influence, there are a number of psychological mechanisms that facilitate and enable these mood changes.

Projections and Other Defense Mechanisms

Sigmund Freud classified *projection* as a defense mechanism operating unconsciously. Projection is an automatic process by which thoughts, motivations, or feelings considered unacceptable by the prevailing (collective) conscious are perceived to exist in others rather than in one's self. Projection also occurs when excessive positive qualities are projected, such as when almost divine characteristics are visualised and imagined onto various idols like leading actors, singers, and sports stars.

Jung regarded the psychological rationale for projections as an archetype that has activated and now seeks expression.[3] He defined the process of projecting as "an unconscious content of the subject . . . is transferred to the object, and there magnifies one of its peculiarities to such proportions that it seems a sufficient cause of disturbance."[4]

Projections have the capacity to create perceptions or imaginary relationships that have little to do with reality, or which provide a much distorted view of reality. Typically, an excessive emotional response is shown towards the particular person, group, object, theme, or situation that is the subject of the projection.

As with many of the other defense mechanisms, the objective of a projection is to reduce anxiety by allowing the venting of unwanted unconscious feelings or impulses without the conscious mind recognising them as such. When undesirable sentiments find an external outlet, the psychological pressure eases and a feeling of relief, a *catharsis*, is achieved. The catharsis tends to legitimise the process of projection as something positive, and this can lead to dire consequences for the targeted individuals, groups, and society as a whole.

It is important to note that we are unlikely to recognise our own projections at work. We use another defense mechanism, *rationalisation*, to explain away or excuse our perception of the targeted scapegoat of our unconscious projections. While those who are the focus of these projections are often quick to realise it, there is little hope of opening the eyes of those doing the projecting. This is because projections usually contain an element of truth to which the projector can cling and tend to exaggerate the basis for their rationalisation.

Projections are possible on both a personal and a collective level, and on the collective level they can give rise to national, even global crises, causing confrontations and wars between groups or countries. The habit of demonising the enemy is typical of war-related propaganda and is one of the most common manifestations of projection-induced behaviour.

Displacement is a related defense mechanism that acts to defuse something considered undesirable by the conscious.[5] The unconscious redirects a feeling triggered by an "unacceptable" person, group, or object into an expression that seeks to find a safe or acceptable outlet. It is a useful mechanism in reducing anxiety when emotions of excessive aggressive or sexual nature are in force, refocusing their expression to outlets considered less threatening by the conscious part of the mind. Displacements can result in somewhat absurd or even dangerous behaviour. For example, aggression may be directed towards an individual or group with a perceived lower hierarchical status than the aggressor; in other words, the aggressor identifies a scapegoat. The displacement reaction is not a means to an end, but is activated through psychological constraints in the conscious part of the mind, which is not able or ready to address the current situation and is seeking a temporary outlet to ease the anxiety.

A variation of displacement is *procrastination*, the act of replacing an important but stressful action with something of a lower priority and which is less stressful, for example, idly surfing the Internet or using social media instead of undertaking a difficult work task. Used as a strategy to cope with anxiety in the conscious mind, procrastination is a sort of temporary denial of reality.

These defense mechanisms activate to handle in the short term anxiety or mental stress arising from the triggering of an archetype, as the conscious is still not ready to handle it. The hallmark behaviours they result in are telltale signs of changes underway in a society's psychological environment. But because the defense mechanisms cannot and do not address the root causes of the anxiety or stress, the pressure on the conscious continues to build up, increasing the risk of neurotic behaviour developing.

The Role of Scapegoats

Groups exposed to projections are commonly referred to as *scapegoats*. Scape-goating can be defined as a "process in which the mechanisms of projection or displacement are utilised in focusing feelings of aggression, hostility, frustration, etc., upon another individual or group; the amount of blame being unwarranted."[6]

Throughout history, scapegoats have included almost every imaginable constellation of people or groups. Whatever the race, nation, gender, sexual orientation, religion, political doctrine or party, corporation, government, or other group or subgroup, if they have been deemed as deviating from what is considered "normal" or acceptable behaviour, they have been the potential target for scapegoating.

Usually, it is the prevailing taboos and attitudes that determine who the scapegoat will be and upon which the archetypal force can act. The scapegoat will be blamed for any mishaps or misfortunes, generally linked to reigning economic, moral, or societal attitudes in force. Demonisation and dehumanisation are frequently used to detach scapegoats from the general community. Dehumanisation can take many forms and can occur at the institutional level down to the individual. It takes various expressions, such as likening the scapegoat to animals ("they live like pigs"), symbolic form, with comparisons to various types of imagery ("they look like pigs"), or physical form, from outright violence down to refusal to make eye contact.[7]

By suppressing our own attitudes and behaviour considered politically incorrect and projecting them onto scapegoats, we comfort ourselves into believing that we are living within society's norms. In the short term at least, this creates an illusory infallibility, but over time it also risks generating neurosis.

Shadow Projections

The negative part of a projection is referred to as a *shadow* projection, and it is the opposite of the ego archetype. Shadow projections reflect taboos, cultural neuroses, and issues considered politically incorrect and not accepted by the ruling societal norms, that is, the collective conscious. However, because these shadow attitudes are an integral part of the holistic mind and are held back in the unconscious, there is a high likelihood that if the repressed material gets too overwhelming as the conscious (self-) censorship becomes too tight, outbursts of shadow projections become likely and an unconscious identification with the scapegoat occurs. It is generally when these conscious, socially acceptable attitudes get tilted out of balance—and when individuals of such a collective start to feel consciously powerless due to these changes—that they become more receptive to the collective shadows that can appear.

As a simple rule of thumb, any attitudes or emotions considered incompatible with existing social standards are the sources that shadow material consists of, and hence can provide clues to which archetypes are likely to activate. So, the more restrictive and narrow a society is from a psychological perspective, the larger is that society's shadow. The contents of the shadow will differ, due to cultural contexts, given that it is projected archetypal images that serve as its representations. However, the format tends to follow similar patterns, on a collective level: verbal forms of hate, rage, witch hunts, and persecutions that usually end in violence of different forms.

Jung distinguishes between a personal and a collective shadow: the collective shadow takes precedence over the individual shadow, the collective shadow provides a broader framework, and the constraints within the individual shadows can evolve.[8]

Zeitgeist

Activation of an archetype brings with it the creation of a general societal mood referred to as zeitgeist, a German word that broadly translates as "the spirit of the age." The zeitgeist provides a narrative and context to the overall cultural, political(-isms), intellectual, mood sentiment, and/or moral ambience for that particular time epoch and collective group.[9] Especially in hindsight, the effects of zeitgeist and the ideas and political or societal trends (such as fashion or other manifestations it produced) can appear as bizarre. They can even take on an almost farcical appearance from today's standards, but they were the norm to which people adhered to in the past.

Historians tend to identify political or economic triggers for the rise of a distinctive zeitgeist, rarely considering or even discussing psychological changes, given the difficulty of assessing and estimating them.

As a zeitgeist is a well-recognised, albeit abstract, concept, it is difficult for historians to exactly pin down when one actually starts and ends, and to describe, in exact forms, its characteristics. However, if zeitgeists can be defined by the archetype that triggers them and establishes their psychological parameters, the analysis can therefore be conducted through the study of archetype-related symbols. The trending of zeitgeists in terms of occurrences can help to gauge timelines and provide a better understanding of the contents, shadows, and related scapegoats.

The narrative of the zeitgeist will help in understanding the particular shifts in public mood and psychic climate. Certain fixed ideas or themes will come to exist within the zeitgeist. These could be collective fantasies directed towards a particular political(-ism) or, from a financial perspective, an investment theme that becomes all the rage, like gold bugs and dot.coms. As these fixations become an embedded part of the collective's perception of reality, they start to trigger action and behaviours to synchronise and align with the gist of the zeitgeist. So what in retrospect might appear to have been absurd statements or decisions made by someone while seized by the zeitgeist were in fact highly rational, under the rigorous context and thought patterns dictated by the zeitgeist. The continuous feeding of a frenzied financial bubble is a typical example of a zeitgeist. Zeitgeists seem to dictate which reality to focus on and what to consciously disregard but unconsciously record; in other

FIGURE 3.1   The Zeitgeist as a Reflection on Reality

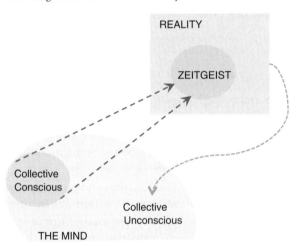

The reigning collective conscious is reflected through the zeitgeist in the way reality is being perceived. Any new information or situation is diagnosed through the constraints of the boundaries set by zeitgeist, and it will also dictate rationality that only can operate within those zeitgeist boundaries.

Any amount or type of reality that does not fit within the context of the reigning zeitgeist due to being considered taboo or due to capacity issues is redirected into the collective unconscious.

words, the zeitgeist encourages turning a blind eye to features of reality or considering reality from a heavily skewed zeitgeist perception. This is the power of the zeitgeist: the discrepancies between psychological illusions that perceive reality lead to a refusal to observe what is in front of us.

And if elements of reality do not corroborate with the world view provided by the zeitgeist, these are ignored or distorted and interpreted not to conflict with the zeitgeist. However, if these elements become too overwhelming and seem to threaten the foundational societal values, the elements cannot only be frowned upon by a conformist public but even be declared "illegal knowledge." History provides plenty of examples, such as the reactions of the leading representatives of the social and cultural values in force at the discovery that the Earth was round and not flat. Another example is Darwin's evolutionary theory. Even today non-conformist findings going against the reigning zeitgeist views can still be subject to such treatment. Highlighted in Figures 3.1, 3.2, and 3.3 is the sequence of archetypal

FIGURE 3.2 A Shift in Reality Leads to the Reigning Zeitgeist Getting out of Synch

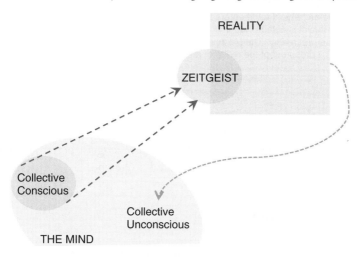

As the reality the zeitgeist was established to best represent shifts, the zeitgeist remains the same; the dislocation between the zeitgeist and reality widens. Some decisions made within the context of the zeitgeist will start to appear as bizarre and unrealistic, especially in hindsight.

As the zeitgeist no longer is ideal to represent the "new" reality, more and more material is suppressed into the unconscious with heightened risk of neurosis and other psychological disturbances.

FIGURE 3.3 An Archetypal Force Replaces the Zeitgeist with Another One That Better Corresponds to Reality

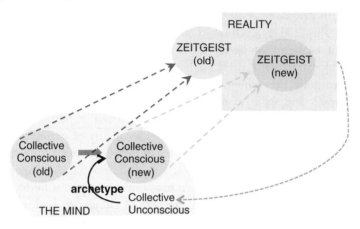

To counter the increased risk of a neurotic mind caused by an unrealistic zeitgeist, an archetype is triggered to better reflect the existing reality. Once the archetypal force enters awareness, a new zeitgeist is established and used as a framework to interpret reality. The old zeitgeist becomes obsolete as it drops out of the realm of reality.

activation as the existing zeitgeist becomes too detached from reality, with the risk of creating neurotic behaviour due to the discrepancies in perceptions and reality. To restore equilibrium, a new zeitgeist better aligned with reality is introduced through the activated archetype.

Mass Hysteria and Panics

When a newly activated archetype starts to make its influence known and comes into direct conflict with the prevailing societal norms and values rather than being complementary, the conflicting sentiments between the conscious and the unconscious can create mass hysteria and panics of various intensity.

Mass hysteria[10] is a collective display of hysterical symptoms, such as unmanageable and excessive exhibits of emotions and loss of self-control, due to overwhelming fear often linked to imagined medical problems or diseases. It tends to coincide with periods of social or economic upheaval. A particularly bizarre form, prevalent in Asia and called *koro*,[11] comes from the fear that men's genitals are shrinking. The symptoms of mass hysteria, referred to as *mass psychogenic illness*[12] or epidemic hysteria, have been extensively studied and psychological stress seems to be a triggering factor. Common features of a hysteric outbreak include the following:

- Symptoms that have no plausible organic basis;
- Symptoms that are transient and benign;
- Symptoms with rapid onset and recovery;
- Occurrence in a segregated group;
- The presence of extraordinary anxiety;
- Symptoms that are spread via sight, sound, or oral communication;
- A spread that moves down the age scale, beginning with older people or those of higher status; and
- A preponderance of female participants.[13]

Other than women being more prone to mass hysteria than men, there is so far no conclusive evidence that identifies any other groups as being more or less likely to be affected. The most typical physical symptoms include headache, dizziness, and nausea.[14]

Hysteria is contagious. It has the capability to spread through non-verbal communication as an automatic and unconscious process. It can also transmit through groups without personal physical contact, such as through e-mail and other social media.[15] The contagion's effects are well noted and recognised in financial markets where sell-off panics are easily triggered and can be due to even unsubstantiated rumours that may spread from market to market, despite no discernible junctions.

This form of contagion has been described as follows:

> When a receiver perceives the emotional expression of the sender, he will automatically imitate these. Through a feedback process the newly adapted emotions will be translated into feelings replicating those of the sender and thus leading to emotional convergence.[16]

Mass hysteria can also spread through a sort of social pecking order, in which people compare their emotional reactions to those of people with a high social status and then adjust their emotions to match.[17]

Another expression of archetypes in direct conflict with the collective conscious is *moral panic*, defined as an increased intensity in negative feelings about issues that are considered to threaten social stability.[18] According to the coiner of the term, the South African sociologist Stanley Cohen (1942–2013), moral panic is triggered when a "condition, episode, person, or group of persons emerges to become defined as a threat to societal values and interests."[19] The person or group accused of threatening the social order is referred to as a *folk devil* (read: scapegoat).[20] The topic of disagreement causing the social disturbance is by definition a social taboo, in other words, something not to be touched upon, publicly at least, and expected to be self-censored. Examples of moral panic include witch hunts, McCarthyism, anti-Semitic pogroms, and Victorian moral reactions to anything sexual. Moral panics include a number of explicit attributes:

Concern. There must be a perceived awareness that the behaviour of the group or category in question is likely to have a negative impact on society.

Hostility. Hostility towards the group in question increases, and they become folk devils. A clear division forms between "them" and "us."

Consensus. Although the concern does not have to be nationwide, there must be widespread acceptance that the group in question poses a very real threat to society. It is important at this stage that the "moral entrepreneurs" are vocal and the "folk devils" appear weak and disorganised.

Disproportionality. The action taken is disproportionate to the actual threat posed by the accused group.

Volatility. Moral panics are highly volatile and tend to disappear as quickly as they appeared, due to a waning in public interest or news reports changing to another topic.[21]

Whereas Jung's focus mainly covered individual patients, he did comment on some specific cases where the activation of an archetype affected the psychological set-up of a whole society. He saw the rise of national socialism in Germany in the 1920s and 1930s as being linked to the archetype *Wotan* (a pagan Germanic wandering god) activated as a psychological compensation for the humiliation suffered by the Germans after World War I. Jung believed that the archetype Wotan's activation led to disturbances in the normal collective consciousness, causing clouded moral judgment. He claimed that the psychological energy of the Wotan archetype drove the development of a new zeitgeist in which moral panics and shadow projections turned the Jewish community into the main scapegoat to take responsibility for a lost war. Furthermore, this zeitgeist allowed for a fanatical demagogue, Adolf Hitler, and a political movement almost exclusively based on scapegoating literally arising out of nowhere to win public support and take power, something which history has shown is a very rare political occurrence.[22]

Conclusion

The activation of an archetype brings with it a number of changes to the psychological environment as part of establishing a new zeitgeist that is better aligned with a changing reality; some of these changes take a more dramatic form, such as hysteria and panics. These sentiments play out at all levels of society, as well as in the financial markets, and can trigger changing trends and price bubbles, which will be reviewed in the following chapter.

Notes

1. Nicholas Lewin, *Jung on War, Politics and Nazi Germany: Archetypes and the Collective Unconscious* (London: Karanc Books, 2009), Chapter 7.
2. Ibid, 198.
3. C. G. Jung, *The Tavistock Lectures* (Vol. 18 in *The Collected Works of C. G. Jung*), ed. R. F. C. Hull, 2nd ed. (Princeton, NJ: Princeton University Press, 1981), par. 352.
4. C. G. Jung, *Collected Works of C. G. Jung Vol. 10*, ed. R. F. C. Hull, 2nd ed. (Princeton, NJ: Princeton University Press, 1981), par. 41.
5. Salman Akhtar, *Comprehensive Dictionary of Psychoanalysis* (London: Karanc Books, 2009), 82.
6. Mondofacto.com, "Scapegoating," www.mondofacto.com/ (accessed November 30, 2013).
7. N. Haslam, "Dehumanization: An Integrative Review," *Personality and Social Psychology Review* 10 (2006): 252–264.
8. Wolf C. Zweig, *Lära känna din Skugga* (Stockholm: Bokförlaget Forum, 1997), 56.
9. Glenn Alexander Magee, "Zeitgeist," *The Hegel Dictionary* (New York: Continuum International Publishing Group, 2011), 262; Robert E. Bartholomew, *Little Green Men, Meowing Nuns and Head-Hunting Panics: A Study of Mass Psychogenic Illness and Social Delusion* (Jefferson, NC: McFarland Publishing, 2001).
10. Robert E. Bartholomew and Erich Goode, "Mass Delusions and Hysterias: Highlights from the Past Millennium," *Committee for Skeptical Inquiry* 24 (May–June 2000), http://www.csicop.org/si/show/mass_delusions_and_hysterias_highlights_from_the_past_millennium (accessed November, 30, 2013).
11. Scott D. Mendelson, *The Great Singapore Penis Panic and the Future of American Mass Hysteria*, CreateSpace Independent Publishing Platform, 2011, www.createspace.com.
12. Weir E. Mass, "Mass Sociogenic Illness," *Canadian Medical Association Journal* 172 (2005): 36.
13. Ibid.
14. Timothy Jones, "Mass Psychogenic Illness: Role of the Individual Physician," *American Family Physician* 62 (2000): 2649–2653, 2655–2666.

15. E. Hatfield, J. T. Cacioppo, and R. L. Rapson, "Emotional Contagion," *Current Directions in Psychological Science* 2 (1993): 96–99.
16. Ibid.
17. G. Schoenewolf, "Emotional Contagion: Behavioral Induction in Individuals and Groups," *Modern Psychoanalysis* 15 (1990): 49–61.
18. Marsha Jones and Emma Jones, *Mass Media (Skills-Based Sociology)* (London: Palgrave Macmillan, 1999).
19. Stanley Cohen, *Folk Devils and Moral Panics: Creation of Mods and Rockers* (St. Albans: Paladin, 1973), 9.
20. Ibid.
21. Jones and Jones, *Mass Media*.
22. C. G. Jung, *Wotan* (Vol. 10 in *The Collected Works of C. G. Jung*), ed. R. F. C. Hull, 2nd ed. (Princeton, NJ: Princeton University Press, 1981), par. 373.

References

Akhtar, Salman. 2009. *Comprehensive Dictionary of Psychoanalysis*. London: Karnac Books.
Bartholomew, Robert E. 2001. *Little Green Men, Meowing Nuns and Head-Hunting Panics: A Study of Mass Psychogenic Illness and Social Delusion*. Jefferson, NC: McFarland Publishing.
Hatfield, E., J. T. Cacioppo, and R. L. Rapson. 1993. "Emotional Contagion." *Current Directions in Psychological Science* 2: 96–99.
Cohen, Stanley. 1973. *Folk Devils and Moral Panics: Creation of Mods and Rockers*. St. Albans: Paladin.
Haslam, N. 2006. "Dehumanization: An Integrative Review." *Personality and Social Psychology Review* 10.
Magee, Glenn Alexander. 2011. "Zeitgeist." In *The Hegel Dictionary*. New York: Continuum International Publishing Group.
Jones, Marsha, and Emma Jones. 1999. *Mass Media (Skills-Based Sociology)*. London: Palgrave Macmillan.
Jones, Timothy. 2000. "Mass Psychogenic Illness: Role of the Individual Physician." *American Family Physician* 62: 2649–2653, 2655–2666.
Jung, C. G. 1981. *The Collected Works of C. G. Jung*. Vol. 10. Translated by R. F. C. Hull. 2nd ed. Princeton, NJ: Princeton University Press.
———. 1981. *The Tavistock Lectures*. Vol. 18 in *The Collected Works of C. G. Jung*. Translated by R. F. C. Hull. 2nd ed. Princeton, NJ: Princeton University Press.
———. 1981. *Wotan*. Vol. 10 in *The Collected Works of C. G. Jung*. Translated by R. F. C. Hull. 2nd ed. Princeton, NJ: Princeton University Press.
Lewin, Nicholas. 2009. *Jung on War, Politics and Nazi Germany: Archetypes and the Collective Unconscious*. London: Karanc Books.
Mass, Weir E. 2005. "Mass Sociogenic Illness." *Canadian Medical Association Journal* 172: 36.
Mendelson, Scott D. 2011. *The Great Singapore Penis Panic and the Future of American Mass Hysteria*. CreateSpace Independent Publishing Platform, www.createspace.com.
Schoenewolf, G. 1990. "Emotional Contagion: Behavioral Induction in Individuals and Groups." *Modern Psychoanalysis* 15: 49–61.
Zweig, Wolf C. 1997. *Lära känna din Skugga*. Stockholm: Bokförlaget Forum.

CHAPTER 4

Archetypal Influences in the Financial Markets

Although Carl Jung never made any specific observations about archetypal influences on the economy or the financial markets, he did occasionally comment on their impact on society as a whole. But the effects he described of activated archetypes on the collective community, such as projections, hysteria, and panics, are easily recognisable features in financial markets.

Financial Bubbles

Financial bubbles are an acknowledged characteristic representing the seemingly recurring folly in financial markets, and occurrences of these bubbles can be traced back to the earliest known speculative markets. The behaviour that causes financial bubbles appears to run counter to the assumptions of human rationality on which most conventional economic doctrine is based.[1] Although investors, financial regulators, and politicians have long been aware of financial bubbles and have at times acted to try to prevent them, while indeed always and indirectly feeding them, financial bubbles still keep occurring, with the propensity to cause grave consequences for society as a whole. It seems that neither an increased investor awareness nor regulatory interference can prevent them from developing. So why, despite the recognition of the risks they bring with them long before they burst, do financial bubbles form? And why do they progress and eventually end in cataclysmic outbursts of hysteria and mass panic despite the increased sophistication of investors, at least superficially, and improved tools to manage and hedge increased financial risks?

Anatomy of a Financial Bubble

Financial bubbles generally begin as increased levels of buying, gradually pushing the price trend higher, later on progressing in a frenzied pace leading to a parabolic price formation, which then eventually crashes in a panic sell-off. The forces at work appear to be driven by herding behaviour, where shared emotions cause an irrational greed that produces upticks that create a self-reinforced momentum, which in turn forms the pattern of a bubble. The collapse of the bubble seems to be driven by the same herding psychological mechanism, which accelerates and plays out a lot quicker than the uptrend, with shared irrational fear driving the sell-off. The average investor, who in isolation might be expected to behave in a rational way, gets lured by and drawn into the thinking of the collective, thus joining and contributing to the behaviour that pumps up the bubble.

For a stock market bubble in particular, characteristics also include extreme levels regarding its valuation, such as the price-earnings (P/E) ratio and the projection of the forward-looking aspects of such valuations, especially if the listed companies currently are not profitable but are by market participants expected to be immensely profitable, normally within a short period of time.

When depicted in a graph (see Figure 4.1), there are generally four recurring phases of the atypical financial bubble:

FIGURE 4.1   A Graphical Depiction of the Different Phases of a Financial Bubble

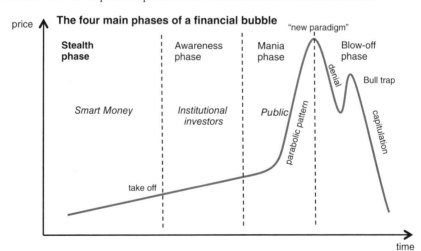

Source: Jean-Paul Rodrigue, available at http://commons.wikimedia.org/wiki/File:
Stages_of_a_bubble.png.

1. **The stealth phase.** An increasing price trend with relatively low participation among the general investment population. The "smart money" begins investing in the market and trade volumes start to rise slowly but surely.
2. **The awareness phase.** The market starts to heat up as institutional investors follow the smart money in growing numbers. Trade volumes further increase and outpace that of the stealth phase. The awareness phase usually sees a minor sell-off before the mania phase kicks in.
3. **The mania phase.** Various media outlets begin to take notice of the rising price trend, bringing it into public awareness and triggering general enthusiasm for the asset. Demand continues to outstrip supply but now in an accelerated pace, further forcing up the price levels. Eventually an all-encompassing greed kicks in with the interest for the particular asset taking a fever-like frenzy, sending the price soaring in a parabolic curve. At the peak of the bubble, to rationally defend the completely unrealistic valuations and prices, there is talk about a "new paradigm" that supersedes traditional approaches to valuing or perceiving the asset. Any critique to the stratospheric price levels are quickly brushed off and can, if seen as persistent, be considered almost blasphemy with the opposing voice being declared as pariah. Trade volumes are at exceptionally high levels during this phase.
4. **The blow-off phase.** Without previous warning "something" happens that switches the market mood; it could be a true or false rumour or a new piece of information. This information may or may not directly relate to the financial asset involved, but is considered at the time to be relevant. The price plunges and the diehard investor collective goes into denial mood. Some of these investors, if not already financially overextended, start to support the price with additional buying; others, maybe late arrivals, see this as a temporarily dip and also chip in and buy. At best, this usually produces just a short uptick and then the price soon starts to fall again, this time with extremely high trade volumes. The bubble, which has taken months or years to grow, collapses in days or weeks, with the majority of investors capitulating and selling at the very bottom. The price of the asset typically falls back to or below the bubble's take-off price level.

Bankruptcy and despair become reality for the investors who were heavily leveraged. The price settles back into the normal mean trend over the next few years. Politicians and financial authorities set up investigations to find out what went wrong and whom to blame. Eventually the investigative committees find some "explanation" and new regulations are introduced to make sure the bubble, in that very asset at least, can never form again.[2]

Underlying Causes of a Financial Bubble

Speculation fuelled by easy access to liquidity is usually blamed for the development of financial bubbles. Indeed, the availability of credit and large reserves of disposable income at hand, usually at a time when interest rates are low, is an important factor, but history has shown that financial bubbles do not always occur under such a situation. There seem to be additional psychological mechanisms at work.[3]

A couple of theories on psychological influences have evolved, but none of them have been conclusively proved. They seem to work as explanatory models for financial bubbles only in terms of the momentum that fuels the bubble but do not explain their origins and root causes and why they end so abruptly. The theories are:

> **The greater fool theory.** An investor makes a speculative purchase of what would rationally be regarded as a dubious investment—that is, through any conventional valuation technique the investment is not worth its current price—with the sole belief that another speculator will come along later and buy it at a higher price.[4]
>
> **Extrapolation.** Essentially a variation of the greater fool theory, in which the investor community extrapolates existing trends, expecting higher prices in the future based exclusively on the belief in the continuation of the existing price trend, leading to over shootings; an upper price deviation versus fair value, obviously extrapolation applies on the way down for the price as well.[5]
>
> **Herding.** The assumption that investors tend to follow the current market trend and buy or sell in the same direction is a cognitive bias that can lead to perceptual distortions. Institutional investors, such as fund managers, are especially prone to herding because of "career risk," ensuring that they do not deviate too far in performance from their peers; the notion is that it is better to be wrong with a high degree of certainty, along with the rest of the industry, than to be right in isolation. So while institutional investors may view purchasing during a bubble as irrational, they continue buying to ensure they stay on track with their benchmark indexes.[6]
>
> A common denominator of these theories is the behaviour of the investors when the financial bubble bursts. They use the *rationalisation*

defense mechanism to support their increasingly absurd behaviour in continuing to buy even as prices have reached senseless levels and they are fully aware of that fact. For example, some will claim to be following a new approach to valuing the assets. And the continuous upward momentum of the price serves as a kind of self-fulfilling prophecy. It confirms that the rationale being used to explain the upward trend is correct, leading to additional buying and further price increases.

Moral hazard. Certain investors, such as those investing other people's money, feel driven to take increased levels of risks to achieve superior performance, because their remuneration is linked to their performance. The higher the risk the investor takes, the higher the potential return for the client and the bigger the payday for the investor. The downside for the money managing investor is generally limited to, at worst, termination of employment and this creates a skewed risk-reward relationship that favours high-risk strategies.[7]

These theories, however, explain the momentum in the uptrend of the financial bubble, not why and when they are occurring, not why a particular asset is subject to a bubble rather than another, and not why and when they eventually burst.

Animal Spirits

Leading economists and investors have long pondered the roots of the seemingly sudden triggering of market euphoria that inflates financial bubbles and the inevitable despair as they are punctured. The English economist John Maynard Keynes (1883–1946) spent much time wrestling with how to kick-start the economy and get it growing again after the severe shock of the stock market crash of 1929 and the subsequent Great Depression. In analysing the Depression, Keynes realised that psychological factors played a decisive role in the decisions of individuals and groups on whether to invest. He called these factors "animal spirits."

> Even apart from the instability due to speculation, there is the instability due to the characteristic of human nature that a large proportion of our positive activities depend on spontaneous optimism rather than mathematical expectations, whether moral or hedonistic or economic. Most, probably, of our decisions to do something positive, the full consequences of which will be drawn out over many days to come, can only be taken as the result of

animal spirits—a spontaneous urge to action rather than inaction, and not as
the outcome of a weighted average of quantitative benefits multiplied by
quantitative probabilities. [Italics added][8]

Keynes believed that swings in the economy and asset prices could be
explained to varying degrees by spontaneous changes in the public mood.
According to him, when animal spirits are low, pessimism dominates, the
pace of investment is slow, and the economy is in the doldrums. Conversely,
when animal spirits are high, naïve optimism prevails along with high levels
of investment—with the risk of asset price bubbles forming. There are
some differing views on where Keynes got the inspiration for the term
"animal spirits"; some claim it stems from the Scottish philosopher David
Hume (1711–1776), regarding his reference to spontaneous motivation,
which derives from the Latin term *spiritus animales*, meaning spirit that
drives human thought, feeling, and action. Others attest to the phrase's
medieval roots.[9]

Keynes was never very specific on the nature of animal spirits and whether
they can be provoked to spring into action. Attempts by politicians and heads
of central banks and others to talk up confidence rarely seem to work. Given
his vagueness on animal spirits, it is not clear what specific direction high levels
of animal spirits will take; that is, will they trigger investments and potential
bubbles in asset X, Y, or Z?

As Keynes and Jung were contemporaries, and Keynes had a well-
documented academic interest in the psychological aspects of economics
and investing, it seems strange that Keynes did not connect his concept of
animal spirits with that of Jung's archetypes. It is almost certain that he was
already aware of Jung's work in the 1920s and 1930s. Some sources point to
the fact that he regarded the unconscious as the root of animal spirits; in his
lecture notes, Keynes wrote the following comment in the paragraph about
animal spirits: "unconscious mental action."[10]

Consumer confidence indexes are sometimes claimed to be a rough proxy
of animal spirits, but whether they actually capture the true essence of animal
spirits is highly questionable, as they hardly ever provide consistent accuracy in
forecasting economic trends such as GDP growth, aggregate investment
growth, and unemployment numbers.

Other economists, especially those focusing on financial crises, such as the
American Hyman Minsky (1919–1996), were convinced that bubbles rise
spontaneously. But neither Minsky nor other economists have been able to
explain the roots of this spontaneity; why is it triggered sometimes and not at
other times, given similar economic contexts and factors?[11]

Keynes' concept of animal spirits received support from the American economists George A. Akerlof and Robert J. Shiller in their 2009 book, *Animal Spirits: How Human Psychology Drives the Economy, and Why It Matters for Global Capitalism*. The authors claim that current research has proved that Keynes' animal spirits are key drivers of economic swings. The two Nobel laureates further develop Keynes' concept by dividing animal spirits into five different aspects:

1. **Confidence**, defined as trust that goes beyond rationality and ranked as the most important of the five;
2. An **aspiration for fairness**, which has the propensity to lead to irrational economic choices;
3. **Corruption** and how the actual awareness of it can in itself lead to recession;
4. **Money illusion**, ignoring or not fully understanding the effects of inflation; and
5. **Narratives** or stories, a kind of zeitgeist that determines and priorities behaviour.

They then back up these five aspects with various examples on how animal spirits play a role in recession, asset price cycles, unemployment, and other economic ills.[12]

However, Akerlof and Shiller are unable to answer the most important questions about animal spirits: Why do certain narratives activate animal spirits while others do not, and why do the levels of confidence fluctuate over time? Nor do they establish a methodology to explain the mechanics of animal spirits and how to forecast them with regards to content and timing.

One of the intellectual fathers of fundamental investing, the American investor Benjamin Graham (1894–1976), introduced the parable of "Mr. Market" to highlight a simple truth: Stock prices will fluctuate substantially versus their perceived fair value.

> Even though the business that the two of you own may have economic characteristics that are stable, *Mr Market's quotations will be anything but. For, sad to say, the poor fellow has incurable emotional problems.* At times he feels euphoric and can see only the favorable factors affecting the business. When in that mood, he names a very high buy-sell price because he fears that you will snap up his interest and rob him of imminent gains. At other times he is depressed and can see nothing but trouble ahead for both the business

and the world. On these occasions he will name a very low price, since he is
terrified that you will unload your interest on him. [Italics added][13]

The Mr. Market parable describes the equity market as a manic-depressive
person, seemingly randomly oscillating between euphoria and depression. The
concept was adopted by Graham's most famous disciple, the American
investor Warren Buffett, who applied the Mr. Market concept as part of
his investment strategy, generally making purchases in the depressive phase of
the stock market.

Corresponding to animal spirits and the Mr. Market idea is the concept of
irrational exuberance, created by Alan Greenspan, the former chairman of the
US Federal Reserve.

> Clearly, sustained low inflation implies less uncertainty about the future,
> and lower risk premiums imply higher prices of stocks and other earning
> assets. We can see that in the inverse relationship exhibited by price/
> earnings ratios and the rate of inflation in the past. *But how do we know
> when irrational exuberance has unduly escalated asset values*, which then
> become subject to unexpected and prolonged contractions as they have in
> Japan over the past decade? [Italics added][14]

Greenspan made this comment during the dot-com bubble and it
was interpreted as a warning that the market had become overvalued. He
evolved of the topic, further retreating from his well-known *laissez-faire* view
of the effectiveness of market forces, recognising that "periodic surges of
euphoria and fear are manifestations of deep-seated aspects of human
nature."[15]

In conclusion, leading economists and investors have recognised and
described the irrational behaviour and shifts in sentiments in financial markets
that lead to outbreaks of hysteria, panic, and unrealistic projections of the
future. But they have made no progress, and largely have remained silent, on
three key questions: Why? How? and When?

An Archetypal Perspective on the Development of Financial Bubbles

Taking a Jungian approach to the formation of financial bubbles (see
Figure 4.2) provides an alternative perspective on its anatomy and gives
insights on timing and pointers on what types of assets that are most prone
to bubble-like behaviour.

FIGURE 4.2 A Jungian Approach to Explain the Anatomy of a Financial Bubble

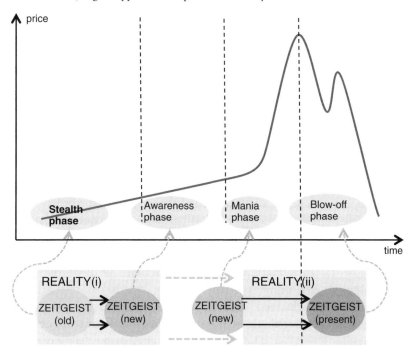

The move from the *stealth phase* to the *awareness phase* represents a shift in zeitgeists, underpinned by the activation of a new archetypal force. The new zeitgeist provides a different perspective on the value of a particular asset, thereby commencing the formation of the bubble. The financial asset in question is selected through the emerging zeitgeist as being the most compatible with the sentiments that this zeitgeist provides. For example, when an archetype such as The Sun becomes active, it releases thought patterns and behaviours that increase the demand for gold-related financial products, as its features share those of the archetype's characteristics. However, note that at inception, the newly formed zeitgeist exists within the realm of reality and the reflection of the asset in terms of pricing and valuation occurs in a "balanced" manner. As time progresses and the sentiments of the new zeitgeist start to attract and influence more investors, reality and zeitgeist eventually diverge and the bubble anatomy enters the *mania phase*.

During the mania phase, the pricing and valuation of the asset become excessive versus historical precedence; however, the investor community keeps buying until prices reach unsustainable levels. Any news, good or bad, whether directly related to the asset or not, is interpreted as a validation of the price level, in fact indicating even higher prices. As the zeitgeist becomes further integrated into the conscious, the belief in the particular asset becomes increasingly dogmatic, and defense mechanisms, such as rationalisation, activate to help explain the unrealistic price; a new economy, a paradigm shift, or similar explanations are used—anything to keep feeding the bubble. Any evidence to the contrary is quickly brushed away and ignored, investors turn a blind eye to anything that can distort the doctrine of an ever-increasing price level. And even if politicians, central bankers, and financial regulators become aware of the bubble formation, the force of the zeitgeist makes their attempts to introduce regulations to stem the speculation frenzy watered down or implemented with so many caveats that the effort lacks effect. It seems that the spell of the archetypal forces has become so strong that even the awareness of a bubble and its consequences cannot be consciously avoided; people with open eyes are drawn to its conclusions and resist any attempts to prevent it, and even if implemented, that awareness is ignored. Thus the introduction of regulations or macroprudent tools in such a psychological environment is meaningless; the forces of the bubble formation can be changed only if the zeitgeist and its psychological foundations can be altered and manipulated. All explanations will be aligned with the reigning zeitgeist. The most ardent proponents of the rationalism of this new paradigm that underpins the financial bubble are generally people most easily susceptible to hysteria or other neurotic conditions.

At the end of the mania phase, there is a distinctly neurotic, almost feverish, relationship between the asset in question and the investor community because the collective conscious is at an unhealthy, imbalanced level. To restore equilibrium in the collective mind, as the distortion between zeitgeist and reality is now at its most extreme, a new archetype is activated to better align with the existing reality. The first signs are spotted through an increase in frequency in symbols related to the new archetype in various media outlets. Shortly after there is a temporary price drop, quite steep in nature, that initiates the *blow-off phase*. This initial price drop causes a "battle" between the archetype that is on its way to dormancy versus the newly activated archetype; consequently, there is thus great confusion in determining the true value of the asset. Eventually, the new archetype establishes itself and the perception is tilted over to a new valuation regime of the asset, a new zeitgeist. While there is a complete breakdown of perceived reality for the investor community and as a consequence the price falls rapidly, a correction of the cognitive dissonance occurs, which triggers a number of defense mechanisms. Some investors go into denial, refusing to believe what is happening, and if they have any funds left, they use them to try to support the price. Others show signs of regression, in a most child-like manner refusing to even look at the latest price quotations, but project their own pains onto a scapegoat, which is by far the most common reaction. As part of reharmonising the equilibrium in the mind and easing the suffering, the blame for the bubble is externalised and projected. The scapegoat usually is a shadow of the newly activated archetype; however, it often has at least a superficial part in the mania phase of the bubble. In the history books, the scapegoat will be pointed out as the cause of the financial bubble.

In a coming chapter, we will explore in detail how to develop a forecasting methodology based on archetypes and their influences on the collective investor mood.

Conclusion

Applying the psychological output from archetypes onto the different phases of a financial bubble provides an alternative explanatory approach to how bubbles form and eventually burst. The distinct psychological manifestations of the activation of an archetype can be timed through studying the performance of its tangible footprints, the symbols. Symbols serve as a prospective forecasting model that an investor could use to profitably time trades in a bubble environment.

Notes

1. *Market Bubbles and Investor Psychology*. Valley Forge, Pa.: Vanguard Group https://institutional.vanguard.com/iam/pdf/VIPS_market_bubbles.pdf (accessed November 30, 2013).
2. Jean-Paul Rodrigue's bio, http://people.hofstra.edu/Jean-paul_Rodrigue/ (accessed November 30, 2013).
3. Ronald R. King, Vernon L. Smith, Arlington W. Williams, and Mark V. van Boening, "The Robustness of Bubbles and Crashes in Experimental Stock Markets," in *Nonlinear Dynamics and Evolutionary Economics*, ed. R. H. Day and P. Chen (New York: Oxford University Press).
4. *Law Dictionary*, "Greater Fool Theory," http://thelawdictionary.org/greater-fool-theory/ (accessed November 30, 2013).
5. Stephen P. Utkus, *Market Bubbles and Investor Psychology* (Valley Forge, PA: Vanguard, 2011).

6. Henry Blodget,"Why Wall Street Always Blows It," *The Atlantic*, December 1, 2008.

7. Allard E. Dembe and Leslie I. Boden, "Moral Hazard: A Question of Morality?" *New Solutions* 10, no. 3 (2000): 257–279.

8. J. M. Keynes, *The General Theory of Employment, Interest and Money* (Create-Space Independent Publishing Platform, 2011, www.createspace.com, 161–162 (accessed November 30, 2013).

9. Matteo Pasquinelli, *Animal Spirits: A Bestiary of the Commons* (Rotterdam: NAi Publishers, 2008).

10. R. C. O. Matthews, "Animal Spirits," *Proceedings of the British Academy* 70 (1984): 212.

11. "Wild-Animal Spirits—Why Is Finance So Unstable? A Special Report on the Future of Finance," *The Economist*, January 22, 2009.

12. George A. Akerlof and Robert J. Shiller, *Animal Spirits: How Human Psychology Drives the Economy, and Why It Matters for Global Capitalism* (Princeton, NJ: Princeton University Press, 2009).

13. Benjamin Graham, *The Intelligent Investor: The Definitive Book on Value Investing. A Book of Practical Counsel*, 7th ed. (New York: HarperBusiness, 2003), Chapter 20.

14. Alan Greenspan, "The Challenge of Central Banking in a Democratic Society," speech given at the American Enterprise Institute, December 5, 1996.

15. Alan Greenspan, *The Age of Turbulence: Adventures in a New World* (New York: Penguin Books, 2008), 520–523.

References

Akerlof, George A., and Robert J. Shiller. 2009. *Animal Spirits: How Human Psychology Drives the Economy, and Why It Matters for Global Capitalism*. Princeton, NJ: Princeton University Press.

Blodget, Henry. 2008. "Why Wall Street Always Blows It." *The Atlantic*, December 1.

Dembe, Allard E., and Leslie I. Boden. 2000. "Moral Hazard: A Question of Morality?" *New Solutions* 10 (3).

The Economist. 2009. "Wild-Animal Spirits—Why Is Finance So Unstable? A Special Report on the Future of Finance," January 22.

Graham, Benjamin. 2003. *The Intelligent Investor: The Definitive Book on Value Investing. A Book of Practical Counsel*. 7th ed. New York: HarperBusiness.

Greenspan, Alan. 2008. *The Age of Turbulence: Adventures in a New World*. Penguin Books.

Keynes, J. M. 2011. *The General Theory of Employment, Interest and Money*. CreateSpace Independent Publishing Platform, www.createspace.com.

King, Ronald R., Vernon L. Smith, Arlington W. Williams, and Mark V. van Boening. 1993. "The Robustness of Bubbles and Crashes in Experimental Stock Markets." In *Nonlinear Dynamics and Evolutionary Economics*, edited by R. H. Day and P. Chen. New York: Oxford University Press.

Law Dictionary. "Greater Fool Theory." http://thelawdictionary.org/greater-fool-theory/ (accessed November 30, 2013).

Matthews, R. C. O."Animal Spirits." *Proceedings of the British Academy* 70: 212.

Pasquinelli, Matteo. 2008. *Animal Spirits: A Bestiary of the Commons.* Rotterdam: NAi Publishers.

Rodrigues, Jean-Paul. Bio. http://people.hofstra.edu/Jean-paul_Rodrigue/.

Utkus, Stephen P. 2011. *Market Bubbles and Investor Psychology.* Valley Forge, PA: Vanguard.

CHAPTER 5

Existing Approaches to Capture Sentiments in Financial Markets, and Why They Do Not Work

Most existing methodologies that aim to capture investor sentiments in the financial markets are built on the theory of *crowd psychology*. This holds that a person in a collective will act differently from, and make decisions significantly different from, how they would think or behave as an individual—even so different that these acts could be in direct conflict. The foundation of crowd psychology assumes that people tend to give up their personal responsibility and surrender to the emotions of a crowd; they feel shielded by the anonymity of the crowd and abandon responsibility. A crowd may therefore assume a life of its own and drive people into behaviour they would otherwise not agree to and even condemn. Crowd psychology focuses on how a crowd as a single entity behaves and acts, as well as how it changes the perceptions of individuals entering the crowd.[1]

Two theories are used to explain the different psychological mindsets of crowds and their individual components: *the convergence theory* and *the contagion theory* (or herding).[2]

According to the convergence theory, it is not the crowd itself that causes crowd behaviour; it is induced by specific individuals with leadership qualities. Thus the name "convergence": the thought patterns and behaviour of individuals drawn to the crowd start to converge with those of the strong-minded leaders of the crowd. As such, crowd behaviour can be considered a rational expression of popular sentiments and values.

In contrast, according to contagion theory, the crowd itself is the catalyst that causes people to act in certain ways. People who share similar beliefs come together and form a collective. Individuals perceived as leaders or of high status take charge and their actions, aligned with the shared beliefs, are imitated by the other members of the group. The crowd behaves like a herd of animals blindly following a few leaders. But the group first coalesces because its members are of a like mind and their views do not change as part of joining the crowd.

The contagion theory was developed in the earliest days of psychology as an academic discipline and has been highlighted by such philosophers as Soren Kierkegaard (1813–1855) and Friedrich Nietzsche (1844–1900) as well as the psychologists Sigmund Freud (1856–1939) and Gustave LeBon (1841–1931), among others.[3] Convergence theory is the more recent of the two theories.

Behavioural Finance

It quickly became evident that the theories underpinning crowd psychology could be applied to financial markets. Many different approaches have evolved and today they are generally grouped under the term *behavioural finance* or the broader *behavioural economics.* [4] The basic tenet of behavioural finance is the influence of emotions on the assumptions of rationality in making financial decisions, which has the tendency to lead to systematic discrepancies. Behavioural finance focuses on three main areas:

1. Inefficiencies in financial markets lead to anomalies and ways of exploiting the arbitrage opportunities that arise, such as the simultaneous buying and selling of related securities with a view to make a riskless profit.
2. Narratives and stereotypes cause myopic behaviour in ways of responding to seemingly similar events.
3. Investors use approximations to override deduction and rationality, which creates trading opportunities.

A lot of research in behavioural finance relates to financial bubbles and the formation of trends due to "excessive" reactions to perceived price-sensitive information. But behavioural finance remains notably silent on why these emotional responses and anomalies arise in the first place, and why trends and bubbles are so variable, in that their occurrences are irregular and they are scattered unevenly among different asset classes.

Technical Analysis

Technical analysis shares its theoretical base with behavioural finance, especially regarding crowd psychology. Its objective is to forecast price trends and directions by studying historical price patterns, in the belief that these repeat over time, and thereby enable profitable trades to be made. Technical analysis draws on the contagion theory; that is, price patterns repeat because the investor collective tends towards similar emotions and behaviour in what are perceived to be recurring and corresponding contexts.

The main tools of technical analysis are price and volume charts, supported by the many indicators and moving averages derived from them. A suite of chart patterns and trends based on price cycles has evolved to gauge investor emotions and the technical analyst applies these to current markets to forecast price moves in the near, medium, and long term.[5]

Does technical analysis work? An extensive range of empirical testing highlights that at best it has delivered mixed results. It seems to work at times and not at others. Applying the different existing methods and techniques to the same market data can produce different conclusions. In setting the parameters used for price forecasting assessments, an element of subjectivity is built into many of the tools and the interpretation of chart patterns. To date, there is no single approach or method that has consistently returned excessive profits at all times.[6]

One approach to technical analysis is *Elliott waves.*[7] It is derived from the *wave principle* developed by the American accountant and chart analyst Ralph Nelson Elliott (1871−1948) in the 1930s based on his study of crowd behaviour, which he claimed followed a recurring rhythmical course. He identified 13 standardised waves that feature both progressive and regressive characters representing optimism and pessimism. The wave patterns have constant forms but could differ in time stretches and breadth. The wave patterns are linked and scalable and therefore are able to form similar larger wave patterns in a fractal manner. According to Elliott, the wave principle could be applied to most activities involving collective human behaviour but his focus remained mainly on the stock markets.

As Elliott pointed to the waves' fractal patterns, he described them in mathematical terms and he identified the *Fibonacci summation series*, an ancient integer sequence popularised by the medieval Italian mathematician Leonardo Pisano Bigollo, also known as Fibonacci (c. 1170−c. 1250), as forming the mathematical basis of the wave principle. Number series from the Fibonacci sequence constitute the building blocks of the various Elliott wave patterns. The Fibonacci sequence is set from 0 and 1 and each following number is the set sum of the previous two. Examples of Fibonacci sequences also appear in nature in tree structures and the formation of snowflakes.

As with other methods of technical analysis, there are elements of subjectivity in how to apply Elliott waves or Fibonacci sequences, making empirical studies inconsistent. Studies made by non-Elliott wave proponents have not been able to identify Fibonacci ratios appearing non-randomly in stock market price series. Another problem is that no clear rules are set for the anchor points of the waves—where they are supposed to start and end—nor for their amplitude, which means there is no single way to apply them on market data and, depending on who does it, trading strategies and their performance can differ significantly.[8]

Efficient Market Hypothesis

There is a school of thought that contrasts with, and contradicts, technical analysis. Called the *efficient market hypothesis* (EMH), it theorises that historical prices cannot be used to make projections about future prices that systematically overperform. Thus it declares void the price patterns and waves proposed by technical analysis. The EMH was developed by the American economist and Nobel laureate Eugene Fama, whose first writing on the topic was published in 1970.[9]

The EMH is based on the assumption that the members of the investor collective have rational expectations, and that on average the collective opinion is correct. Whenever new price-sensitive information appears, members of the investor collective revise their expectations. Some may overreact to this new information, others may underreact, but their reactions are random and follow a normal distribution pattern. So the EMH concludes that the net effect on market prices cannot be reliably exploited to make an abnormal profit.

There are three levels of market efficiency under the EMH: weak, semi-strong, and strong. The *weak level* holds that publicly traded asset prices already reflect all publicly available information, so future prices will be determined entirely by information not included in existing prices. Therefore, their movement will be random—they follow what is called a *random walk*. In essence, future prices cannot be projected based on analysis of historical prices, as there exist no autocorrelation so that recurring price patterns can establish themselves. Under this condition, technical analysis cannot provide systematic excess returns.

The *semi-strong level* holds that in addition to reflecting all publicly available information, asset prices adjust quickly to new publicly available information.

The *strong level* holds that as well as reflecting all publicly available information, asset prices also immediately adjust to insider information—privately held information about the asset—so a price reflects all information, both public and private.

Academics and investor professionals have tested the validity of the EMH on various markets since publication of the hypothesis in 1970. Tests include autocorrelation tests (to ensure that stock market returns are not significantly correlated over time) as well as testing whether stock price changes are independent over time. For the semi-strong form of EMH, testing also incorporates testing for price adjustments due to new price sensitive information being made available, such as earnings releases.

For the strongest form of EMH, accurate testing becomes more difficult, although insiders have to flag and report any purchases and no evidence of systematic overperformance can be demonstrated following these *legal* insider transactions; however, the identification of any *illegal* insider transactions are obviously more difficult to keep track of, as these are not reported through financial authorities or the transactions are conducted through third-party proxies.

The general conclusion on whether markets are efficient is: for most of the time, yes, but not always. A number of anomalies exist; for example, few are denying the fact of trending markets. That is, yesterday's prices generally influence today's price level; hence, it does not seem that prices always follow a random walk because occurrences of momentum effects can occasionally be observed. But applying the tools of technical analysis, based on historical price patterns, will work only part of the time, because it is also noted that the markets do not always follow trends. Therefore, one cannot consistently achieve returns in excess of market average, given the information available at the time the investment is made. Such price patterns should, according to the EMH, evaporate as investors notice them and trade in advance until the price discrepancy fizzles out.

Some of the existing and persisting anomalies relate to slower-than-expected adjustments after earnings releases. The price does not immediately adjust to the new information but instead drifts over time until it reaches its new equilibrium, which distorts the theory of an efficient market. This is explained by the EMH camp as overreaction to news; however, since it was first noted in 1968, this effect is still observable and it is possible to commercially exploit it in different markets. There are other momentum effects relating to specific dates of the calendar, valuation, and market capitalisation of stocks that seem to persist over time, despite being well documented and known among investors.

Regarding financial bubbles, EMH proponents say that at the time of a bubble, the price level is considered rational and it is only really in hindsight that bubbles are defined. Accordingly, this explanation maintains the integrity of the EMH. However, mainstream academics and financial professionals point to the existence of financial bubbles as a challenge to the validity of the EMH, especially in the aftermath of the bubbles in the last few years, which have raised serious question marks about markets' abilities to accurately reflect the risks in the underlying economy.

The following issue is rarely raised: Why are markets efficient sometimes and not at other times, and is there a way to forecast the different levels of efficiency?

Black Swans

The author Nassim Nicolas Taleb coined the term *black swans*, meaning key events that in finance would be represented by crashes in the financial markets but also would include significant historical and political milestones with the common denominator that they seemingly occur without warning and are impossible to predict. Explanations in hindsight are often rationalisations and over-simplifications of complex events. Taleb argues that because these events occur only rarely they become difficult to assign probabilities to in terms of likelihood and outcomes and as such, even implicitly, are excluded from normal anticipations and scenario planning. He concludes that predicting these black swan events is not possible, but Taleb maintains that as a precautionary measure, one can at least prepare oneself to estimate price risks not through normal distributions but through distributions that incorporate long tails to capture the outcome of rare events. Obviously, he concludes that such measures will not help in timing black swan events, nor will they help to explain for what particular asset they can occur or the origin of the event. Taleb, however, never considers nor discusses changes in the overall psychological sentiments as a possible explanatory model to sudden drastic switches in investor perception or other societal regime shifts.[10]

Social Mood

Socionomics,[11] a branch of behavioural finance, provides another way of explaining trends and financial bubbles that seem to defy rational behaviour. The American financial analyst Robert Prechter established the premise of socionomics in 1979 and has been working on it ever since. He sees a society's general social mood as the precursor to social action. He uses indexes of the major asset prices as a tool to measure the public's general mood, a tool he calls a *sociometer.* The single number of a financial index, such as the S&P500, is a measure of sentiment about future prospects, and major changes in trends represent mood swings among a broader population, not all of whom are investing in the particular index. Prechter believes that a general collective optimism in society is reflected through uptrending stock markets, while a pessimistic mood is represented by falling stock markets. The bigger the upward or downward trend swings, the greater the intensity of the collective optimism or pessimism. According to Prechter, a financial index is a better gauge of social mood than other indicators, such as surveys, because it provides a consistent measurement. Given that a financial index produces a single number, it can be tracked back over a reasonably long time, and it is frequently updated, lending itself better to analysis and statistical testing through its time series.

While it is commonly assumed that societal and economic trends and events, including war and movements in politics, affect people's moods as well as their attitudes towards investing, socionomics reverses the chain. Prechter says it is the social mood that causes societal and economic cycles, wars, and other collective human tendencies. But he remains elusive on the source of social moods, other than referring to them as a natural product of human interaction.

Prechter's waxing and waning social moods fit in with the principle of Elliott waves. So, social moods, in accordance with Elliott waves, determine the traits and duration of various social trends, whether related to financial markets, culture, or politics. In essence, social moods govern events and social activity; human behaviour changes as a result of internal psychological forces, not external ones. The interpretation of social moods from a rising stock market would indicate general times of peace and social harmony, for example, more children being born, whereas a falling stock market would indicate a negative social mood and serve as a precursor to social conflicts and war. Obviously natural disasters are not influenced by social moods, but Prechter makes the point that epidemics of disease can be influenced by social moods.

So what is the internal force driving the social mood? Prechter points to the herding behaviour lurking in the unconscious, which defies the rational thinking tenets of conventional economics. He sees the social mood in a continuous state of flux between negative and positive, so it is essentially a bipolar force that oscilliates between the two extremes. The response to the social mood comes in two types: (1) collective action, in which the members of a group act together, for example, in riots or demonstrations; and (2) aggregate action, which is the sum of individual activity, such as trends in stock markets or fashion. Both types follow Elliott wave patterns and can, according to followers of socionomics, thus be forecasted by applying the standardised set of patterns onto the levels of financial indexes.

Advocates of socionomics use it to make projections not only regarding investments but also social events and trends, more as a rough and anecdotal, rather than precise, guide to the unfolding of events.

More important, Prechter seeks a difference between *moods* and *emotions.* He defines emotions as "exogenously referred, consciously experienced feelings, regulated by a combination of mood, conditions and events. Mood is an endogenously regulated, unconsciously experienced mental state, managed by Elliott waves. Mood predisposes people toward certain emotions."[12]

Socionomists apply three primary time scales for social behaviours:

1. **Short-term events**. A few weeks/months to a few years.
2. **Medium-term events**. A few years to a decade or two.
3. **Long-term events**. A few decades to a few centuries.[13]

Because the pattern foundation of socionomics is based on Elliott waves, it suffers from the same lack of precision in establishing starting points for wave movements. It is also limiting in that moods come in only two flavours: positive and negative, which limits the type of forecasts one can do, other than more generally representing the two corresponding moods. Socionomics does not give clues to the character and finer aspects of social mood. Also within the socionomics community, key questions remain unanswered about the exact nature and source of mood formation:

> A huge question, of course, is how exactly this mood formation takes place in a highly heterogenous population. That is still a deep answered research question. It's reasonable to assume that the answer is bound-up with the types of "transmitters" and "receivers" in the society and the way they interact. But that's not saying much. What matters is the specific way these factors line up to create a sharp change of mood, a kind of "phase transition" from one social mood to another.[14]

Emotion Words

As new online social media have been introduced over the last few years, it has become possible for researchers to access *Big Data*, collections of huge and increasingly complex data sets, so that normal approaches to database management and analysis become difficult to conduct. The benefit of analysing such large data sets is that it is now feasible to detect patterns that might be hidden if only using samples or limited selections of data, and that any statistical findings can now be determined with greater confidence.

A research team from Indiana University and University of Manchester[15] gathered *emotion words* from a broad collation of Twitter accounts and devised a methodology to define mood in six different dimensions (*Calm, Alert, Sure, Vital, Kind,* and *Happy*) by developing a dictionary that provided categorisation onto these dimensions. The central tenet of the testing was that large samples of emotion words would represent the collective mood and use the number of emotions words to predict daily moves in the Dow Jones Industrial Average Index from two to six days later. They thought that by large-scale reviewing tweets, with their 140-character limit, they would draw out the gist of individuals' daily moods. However, they acknowledged the definition problems with natural languages including ambiguity, irony, double meanings, and word puns. Their claim was that this prediction model gave an 87.6 percent accuracy in forecasting the short-term moves of Dow Jones.

On the back of this research, *Derwent Capital* established a hedge fund and trading platform that would use Twitter sentiments to make investments and developed a specific algorithm to trade in multiple markets. However, the hedge fund was liquidated within a month of commencement and its trading platform has also folded, which of course questions the predictive qualities of the forecasting model, whether based on theoretical deficiencies of the model and/or the implementation thereof. Meantime, a new attempt to launch a similar venture is underway.[16,17]

Conclusion

Existing methodologies that aim to describe and forecast the investor sentiments that underpin trends and financial bubbles appear to be lacking; their projective capabilities have proven lackluster. What seems to be the switch between rational and irrational behaviour among the investor collective requires a dynamic effort in a modelling attempt that considers influences from the collective unconscious.

Notes

1. "Crowd Psychology," in *Blackwell Encyclopedia of Social Psychology*, ed. A. S. R. Manstead and M. Hewstone (Oxford, UK: Blackwell, 1996), 152–156.
2. "What Is Crowd Psychology?" www.wisegeek.com, (accessed November 30, 2013).
3. M. S. Greenberg, "Crowd psychology," in *The Corsini Encyclopedia of Psychology*, 4th ed., ed. Irving B. Weiner and W. Edward Craighead (Hoboken, NJ: John Wiley & Sons, 2010).
4. "Behavioural economics," *The New Palgrave Dictionary of Economics Online* (2008). www.dictionaryofeconomics.com/dictionary (accessed November 30, 2013).
5. Charles D. Kirkpatrick and Julie Dahlquist, *Technical Analysis: The Complete Resource for Financial Market Technicians* (Upper Saddle River, NJ: FTPress, 2006).
6. Gunduz Caginalp and Henry Laurent, "The Predictive Power of Price Patterns," *Applied Mathematical Finance* 5 (1998): 181–206.
7. M. Poterba and L. H. Summers, "Mean Reversion in Stock Prices: Evidence and Implications," *Journal of Financial Economics* 22 (1988): 27–59; C. Heol-Ho Park and Scott H. Irwin, "The Profitability of Technical Analysis: A Review," AgMAS Project Research Report no. 2004–047; Ralph Nelson Elliott, *R. N. Elliott's Masterworks*, ed. Robert R. Prechter Jr. (Gainesville, GA: New Classics Library, 1994).
8. Ibid.
9. Justin Fox, *Myth of the Rational Market* (New York: HarperBusiness, 2009); Joe Nocera, "Poking Holes in a Theory on Markets," *New York Times*, June 5, 2009.
10. Nassim Nicholas Taleb, *The Black Swan: The Impact of the Highly Improbable*, 2nd ed. (New York: Random House Trade Paperbacks, 2010).
11. Robert R. Prechter Jr., *Socionomics: The Science of History and Social Prediction* (New York: New Classics Library, 2003).
12. An interview with Robert R. Prechter Jr., "Where I Believe Socionomics Is Heading," *Socionomist* June 2010.
13. John L. Casti, "Mood Matters, from Rising Skirt Lengths to the Collapse of World Powers," *Copernicus* 15 (2010).
14. Ibid., 17.
15. Johan Bollen, Huina Mao, and Xiao-Jun Zeng, "Twitter Mood Predicts the Stock Market," *Journal of Computational Science* 2, no. 1 (March 2011): 1–8.
16. "Last Tweet for Derwent's Absolute Return," *Financial Times*, May 24, 2012.
17. Cayman Atlantic, www.caymanatlantic.com/twitter-trading/4577095193 (accessed November 30, 2013).

References

Bollen, Johan, Huina Mao, and Xiao-Jun Zeng. 2011. "Twitter Mood Predicts the Stock Market." *Journal of Computational Science* 2, no. 1 (March): 1–8.

Gunduz Caginalp and Henry Laurent. 1998. "The Predictive Power of Price Patterns." *Applied Mathematical Finance* 5.

Casti, John L. 2010. "Mood Matters, from Rising Skirt Lengths to the Collapse of World Powers." *Copernicus* 15.

Cayman Atlantic. 2013. www.caymanatlantic.com/twitter-trading/4577095193.

"Crowd Psychology." 1996. In *Blackwell Encyclopedia of Social Psychology*. Edited by A. S. R. Manstead and M. Hewstone. Oxford, UK: Blackwell: 152–156.

Fox, Justin. 2009. *Myth of the Rational Market*. New York: HarperBusiness.

Greenberg, M. S. 2010. *Corsini Encyclopedia of Psychology*. "Crowd psychology."

Charles D. Kirkpatrick and Julie Dahlquist. 2006. *Technical Analysis: The Complete Resource for Financial Market Technicians*. Upper Saddle River, NJ: FT Press.

"Last Tweet for Derwent's Absolute Return." 2012. *Financial Times*, May 24.

Manstead, ASK;Hewstone, Miles. 1996. *Blackwell Encyclopedia of Social Psychology*. Oxford, UK: Blackwell.

The New Palgrave Dictionary of Economics Online. 2008. "Behavioural economics."

Nocera, Joe. 2009. "Poking Holes in a Theory on Markets." *New York Times*, June 5.

Park, Cheol-Ho., and Scott H. Irwin. 2004. "The Profitability of Technical Analysis: A Review." AgMAS Project Research Report no. 2004–04.

Poterba, M., and L. H. Summers. 1988. "Mean Reversion in Stock Prices: Evidence and Implications." *Journal of Financial Economics* 22.

Prechter, Robert R., Jr., 2003. *Socionomics: The Science of History and Social Prediction*. New York: New Classics Library.

Prechter, Robert R., Jr., 2010. "Where I Believe Socionomics Is Heading." Interview. *The Socionomist*, June.

Taleb, Nassim Nicholas. 2010. *The Black Swan: The Impact of the Highly Improbable*. 2nd ed. New York: Random House Trade Paperbacks.

"What Is Crowd Psychology?" 2013. www.wisegeek.com.

CHAPTER 6

Developing a Conceptual Measurement Methodology Based on Archetypal Forces

Part I: Building Blocks

Chapter 5 highlighted a number of standard theories—some nowadays considered defunct, others still in vogue—used to explain the psychological drivers behind price trends and, especially, the occurrence of bubbles in financial markets. The generic problem with all these methodologies is that they, at best, seem applicable only occasionally and no one has been able to explain and predict when they are more likely to work or why they work. The collective investor sentiments driving these market forces just seem too elusive to be captured by standard models. The perceived irrationality in making investment decisions appears difficult to time and the existing methodologies fail to provide a convincing rationale concerning the triggers and root causes. Typically these psychological triggers are often quickly glossed over as "stemming from the unconscious" or leisurely referred to as "animal spirits" with no further in-depth explanation.

Given the huge impact these fluctuations have on asset prices, and society at large, as financial bubbles over and over highlight, and the fact that fundamental valuation models do not factor them in at all, it is important to try to understand the nature of the underlying drivers. So, if an approach based on recurring price patterns, the trending of "emotion words," or any other attempts to capture and predict investor sentiments do not seem to be viable explanatory models, is there another way?

Adopting an approach that recognises the influences of Jungian archetypes as an explanatory methodology to the trends, fads, hysteria, and panics that occur in the financial markets could prove a viable path, as it would help to explain the apparently spontaneous outbursts of irrational behaviour from the perspective of the conscious. Given the characteristics of archetypes and how they, when activated, influence collective human behaviour, they could provide a succinct explanation to the seemingly infrequent bubbles and why it is so hard to break out of the spell of bubbles even when recognising them. As the archetype-related zeitgeists induce constraints in rational thinking that is limited by its boundaries, certain parts of reality are dimmed out, because they do not fit within the context of the reigning zeitgeist. Regardless of news relating to the asset, this mindset will apply an archetype-bound filter to fit the perspective of the zeitgeist. In other words, if the zeitgeist is aligned with the asset gold, the mindset induced by the archetype will discriminate against any negative views on gold as a preferred asset.

From the standpoint of statistical outcomes, the following objectives are foremost when developing a forecasting model based on archetypal forces:

• To establish that an archetype has activated through a noted increase in the frequency of proxy symbols, in excess of a preset threshold, throughout a broad variety of media, and that the activated archetype represents a change in the psychological environment; and
• To calculate the probability that a particular activated archetype will trigger collective thought patterns that dictate the investment behaviour which guides the specific trend direction for a certain asset. This calculation must be established on historical correlation patterns between the increased occurrences of archetype-related symbol appearances and moves in the corresponding assets, within a specified time lag, and with a high degree of probability.

Note that an increasing trend of symbol occurrences in media outlets need not be followed by a matching pattern in the price of the asset; that is, the price could be falling as well as rising. Furthermore, the relative magnitude of the moves also need not be mirroring. Typically the depicted characteristics of the moves tend not to be identical, as the archetypal activation takes the form of a sudden outburst or spike, whereas the trend of a financial asset generally has a less steep incline; however, its decline can be more drastic. As such, a 500 percent increase of symbol words need not be followed by a 500 percent increase in price for the financial asset. In fact, it is likely to be of a much lower magnitude, although through our testing we have as yet to identify any power laws. Nor is there any resemblance in terms of time duration with the symbol words spike occurring over a few weeks or months, with, in general, multiple year-long trends for the matching financial asset.

However, constants need to be established with regards to distance in time between an uptrend in symbol words and a major move in price for the asset in question. Only minor variations in terms of time for these constants can be allowed for a link between the move in symbols and a price trend to qualify as "valid." One must also, a priori, establish what constitutes a major price move both in regards to relative changes in terms of percentages and time duration to determine the success ratio of the relationship between symbol words and asset prices. The forecast model should ideally also be able to project when the particular price trend is likely to end. An example of a valid symbol signal would be that repeated historical pattern of a suite of Sun-related symbols that shows a frequency spike in excess of 300 percent, and that within two to three weeks there is an 80 percent likelihood that the gold price will initiate an increasing price trend of 15 to 25 percent that will conclude over the next three months.

To ensure consistency in the testing, applying a standardised symbol dictionary on the same data sources, with the same filters and relativisation rules, must provide exactly the same symbol time series regardless of who is performing the analysis. If these conditions are in place, the forecasting methodology lends itself to empirical testing and verification, which will ensure accuracy in terms of identical data extractions when repeated.

To classify any forecasting methodology as successful, it needs to produce, with the described conditions being in place, over time, an over-performance; that is, the statistical probability of recurring relationships between the related symbol words and asset prices must beat the correlation with any random election of sample words with a significant proportion. As far as possible, prior to testing, archetypes need to be pinned to their naturally linked financial assets, like that of the archetype The Sun to gold, the archetype The Mother to low levels of the fear index, VIX, and so on. As a first level of hypothesis testing these relations needs to be verified at some level. In addition, randomly selected words not deemed to hold a symbolic meaning need to be included in order to calculate the probability of random correlations to financial assets. These random selections are set as "noise" benchmarks to be compared with the legitimate symbol words.

Some of the methodological questions that need to be answered include the following: If archetypes activate individually or need to be clustered in narratives, does one model of archetypes stand alone or do archetypal characters combine with settings, activities, and descriptions to then play out in sequences as part of thematic patterns or stories? Can different archetypes be active in parallel, thus independently affecting different asset classes or could they cause push and pull factors in determining price levels? Can archetypes be nested within archetypes activated through clusters on shorter time frames and give rise to counter trends within a larger trend? Can archetypes accentuate an existing trend's magnitude? What are the general time frames in which archetypes play out? Could the time frame include everything from decades down to days?

Linking Symbols to Archetypes

Obviously, statistical testing between time series will only be able to provide levels of correlation, not causality. Causality comes with the definitive conclusive neuroscientific evidence of an archetypal structure in the mind and proof of its influence on human behaviour and their manifestations through symbols. Such conclusive evidence has not in its entirety yet been demonstrated, although a plethora of anecdotal evidence now points to its existence and merits establishing the hypothesis of archetypal influences on human behaviour through the assumption that its activities can be captured through symbols. It seems that the better science understands the functionality of the brain and its relation to the mind, and with progressing research, the stronger the hypothesis of archetype influence. The use of symbols as a communication and impacting tool of the unconscious is better evidenced through empirical testing, especially at the individual level. However, even if it is possible to demonstrate a strong correlation between certain themes of symbols that provide a statistically valid and commercially exploitable early warning signal, one still cannot be entirely certain of a causal relationship. Unfortunately, the final evidence for actual brain patterns or activities triggering such an archetypal thought pattern is still not there. Therefore, establishing strong leading correlation between predefined archetypal symbols and investment strategies comes with a decisively unproved causality link. However, as tests are conducted to reduce the likelihood of random moves and to ensure consistency in correlation patterns over time, we gain at least circumstantial evidence of certain symbols' precursory power to the framing of the mind leading to specific investment decisions.

Once the universe of symbols is defined, they are categorised and attributed to the population of archetypes in a composite manner providing descriptions of the archetypes. Archetypes can be grouped as characters, situations, and objects, so symbols must be selected to reflect the individual archetypal facets. Symbols related to archetypes therefore count in the hundreds but once they have been mapped to archetypes, they remain fixed as the archetypal characteristics do not change. Of course regular screens must be conducted to add newly introduced synonyms to both symbols and archetypes. When the mapping has been established, the pull of data out of the media sources becomes mechanical in nature and minimises the likelihood of subjectivity.

The linking of symbols to archetypes ultimately rests on the foundations that people's language reveals their mindset, even if implicitly and sub-liminally. Furthermore, various symbols are used to describe reality trends over time in terms of themes due to changes in thought patterns in the unconscious and come to represent a zeitgeist that influences and colours perceptions of reality.

The only way to tangibly observe archetypal forces at work is through the symbols they produce. The basic assumption is that once an archetype activates from a dormant state, this shift can be registered through a noted increase in the frequency of symbols, words, or other objects related to the particular archetype through a continuous monitoring of data sources—all-inclusive enough to represent the collective unconscious. Typically the symbol occurrences will dramatically increase as the archetypal force begins to transcend into awareness. Once the archetypal force starts to recede, this will be represented through a similar downturn in symbol frequency. Plotted on a chart, the particular symbol frequency will form a spike. Eventually the archetype will return to its dormant state and the related symbol words will yet again become background noise, indistinguishable from any randomly selected words in terms of frequency. However, they need not necessarily drop to zero occurrences. Subsequently, through the symbols, if correctly mapped, it will be possible, in a composite structure, to track the intensity of archetypes and make forecasts in terms of investment decisions, their timings, directions, and possibly scales based on earlier empirically tested statistical relationships between symbol activity and moves in prices in various financial assets. By zooming in on the fluctuations of the symbols related to the various arche-types, we gain a microscopic view on sentiments that reside below the levels of consciousness. The benefit of pinning down archetypes to the regular count of symbols is the objectivity it provides. It comes down to a single number that over time can be developed into a time series that lends itself to statistical testing and validation, versus a time series of asset prices, because such a stability is provided in the methodology. Figure 6.1 provides a schematic that depicts the links between archetypes through symbols on price fluctuations in financial assets.

FIGURE 6.1   A Depiction Highlighting the Links between Archetypes through Symbols and Volatility in Financial Assets

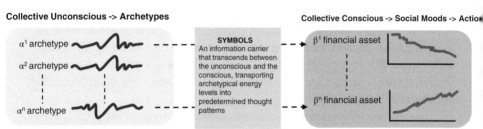

The links between specific archetypes, attributed symbols, and financial asset goes through causal analysis, correlation testing, and calibrations

Capturing Symbols

There are a number of approaches used in capturing symbols because they appear in a variety of contexts, although mostly in text formats. When extracting symbol words as representations of archetypes, it is pivotal to do so only when the word is used in its figurative meaning rather than its literal meaning, as a lack of filtering will contaminate and distort true signals. It is only then that they convey the archetypal energy and influences from the collective unconscious.

Grammatically, symbol words need to be broken down and categorised into subjects, verbs, objects, and adjectives to facilitate the development of a composite index best reflecting the specific characteristics of the archetype.

Assessing the suitability of each forum where symbol words typically appear and the different ways they manifest in these forums will facilitate the selection of the most suitable data sources. The various approaches used to capture symbols include the following:

- Active imagination
- Dreams
- Intuition
- Freudian slips
- Metaphors
- Myths, legends, and sagas
- Taboos

Active Imagination

Active imagination is a method of assimilating unconscious contents, presented as self-expressions by stimulating fantasies and imagination through focused concentration, in other words, a kind of dreaming with open eyes. Although it is generally done in consultation with a psychoanalyst as part of therapy sessions, it can also take place spontaneously. Jung deployed active imagination as a meditation technique to draw out contents from a patient's unconscious. The content generally manifests in the form of images and narratives, from which symbols can be identified and noted for analysis.[1] Because the technique is performed individually, its main focus is the therapeutic work on the personal unconscious rather than the collective unconscious, although elements of the collective unconscious will also be represented. To incorporate active imagination as part of a symbol measurement methodology has certain constraints:

- The symbolic representations from the collective unconscious must be segregated from the ones harboured in the personal unconscious. To ensure such filtering one needs to be able to gather data from a wide and varied population with regards to gender, age, cognitive ability, culture, race, and other characteristics to ensure that one captures the common denominators among these individuals, thus representing the collective unconscious and filtering out the individuals' personal elements.
- There is also the obvious problem with an objective interpretation of these subjective symbol displays in the fashion various individuals describe them and ensuring that the interpretations can be standardised to avoid ambiguities.
- Other problem areas include determining how to objectively assess the magnitudes of symbol occurrences, as they will not readily lend themselves to a simple count, and the fact that the updating of data needs to be done with a regular frequency. Biannual or annual measurement points would be too infrequent and would lead to data points too scarce to develop a time series that lends itself to statistical testing.

The practical problems with setting up a population of individuals willing to participate in an active imagination exercise and report on a regular basis and the cleansing, count standardisation, and ascertaining of objectivity makes active imagination a cumbersome and less feasible option for a data collection methodology.

Dreams

Dreams are defined by psychoanalysts as independent and spontaneous manifestations of the unconscious.[2] Jung considered dreams to be symbolic depictions of the current situation in the mind from the point of view of the unconscious. Through his empirical work with patients, he recognised that many dreams are not in accord with the conscious mind. Indeed, many of his patients' dreams, as well as his own, often seemed out of whack with experiences in daily life. His assumption was that these dreams stemmed from the unconscious. To Jung, this was further evidence of the autonomy of the unconscious, as such dreams cannot be influenced by the conscious since they appear outside our control.[3] He considered these unconscious types of dreams as a psychological device that helps to self-regulate the mind; if the conscious attitude has become too one-sided, then dreams stemming from the unconscious take a contrasting or complementary side to help restore psychological equilibrium.[4] The number of unconscious dreams will therefore increase at times when the conscious part of the mind needs to be pushed back to achieve a holistic balance.

Dreams have always been the traditionally preferred method that psychoanalysts use in the study of the unconscious and its symbols. However, as with active imagination, dreams are studied from the individual perspective rather than the collective. Therefore, dreams also come with the disadvantage of meshing symbols from both the personal and the collective unconscious. Unless dreams can be collated from a broader sample of individuals to distinguish common features, the risk of contamination is obvious. Thus, for purposes of measurement, as with active imagination, dreams are unsuitable as a collection methodology of symbols.

Intuition

Intuition is commonly defined as "the ability to acquire knowledge without the use of reason."[5] Intuition stems from the Latin word *intueri*, which can be translated as "to look inside."[6] Colloquially, it is often referred to as "a gut feeling"; in essence, knowing something without being able to justify it. Jung took great interest in intuition, labeling it "perception via the unconscious."[7] He viewed intuition as the unconscious' way to provide ideas and possibilities out of a blocked situation that the conscious part of the mind is not equipped to handle. Therefore, an increase in the occurrences of intuition should coincide with the need to ensure a psychological equilibrium in the mind and the likely activation of an archetype.

Scientifically, intuition is often described as an unconscious recognition memory, to highlight the fact that intuition arises from information that has been processed and can be retrieved but that has never entered conscious awareness.[8]

And although intuition is a direct tap into the unconscious with the possibility to observe and document symbolic contents, it is a less suitable source as it is difficult to collate large numbers of intuition occurrences over larger samples of the population. Even if an increase in numbers of intuition events can be equated as an increase in activities in the unconscious, it is not necessarily so that the intuition occurrences in themselves will produce symbols that will provide clues on which specific archetypes have been activated.

Because intuition is difficult to provoke deliberately and is context-dependent, in terms of data pulling, it is most likely to source its content from the personal unconscious rather than the collective, since it is individually driven.

Freudian Slips

In Sigmund Freud's book *The Psychopathology of Everyday Life*, he introduces the concept of *parapraxis* (or in Freud's original German, *Fehlleistung*), now commonly known as *Freudian slips*.[9] He defines Freudian slips as seemingly innocent and accidental mistakes, usually of speech, but which actually represent an unconscious thought, belief, or wish that is suppressed by the reigning societal norms. Examples of Freudian slips include the following:

- Forgetting people's names;
- Forgetting something one intended to do;
- Slips of the tongue or pen;
- Losing or temporarily mislaying things;
- Bungled accidents; and
- Remembering things inaccurately.[10]

According to Freud, studying these unconscious, deliberate slips helps to understand the true intentions of a person who is being held back by conscious considerations.

He also expanded this concept to apply to jokes, in that jokes served as an outlet to express things not normally accepted by society; that is, in today's terms something seen as politically incorrect but that in the right humouristic context, disguised perhaps using euphemisms or word puns, could be regarded as an acceptable expression of suppressed contents. He noted that the telling of such jokes produces a sudden release of pent-up energy derived from the release of libido from the unconscious. Freud was particularly interested in studying jokes of a sexual nature as he was working during the Victorian area, when anything related to sexuality was considered taboo.[11]

Many jokes are structured around *irony*, *word plays*, or *double entendres* to deliver the humorous effect through drawing out absurdities from intentionally ambiguous words or sentences to highlight contents not considered acceptable by the existing societal norms.

Can Freudian slips be used as a mechanism to identify symbol words? Because the key source for the collation effort is text material, it will contain few cases of Freudian slips because they are generally edited away, except perhaps in items such as interview transcripts. The detection of Freudian slips through filter rules becomes hard given their lack of specific markers denoting them as Freudian slips. It is the use of symbol words in jokes or other figurative language rather than the meaning of the jokes themselves, unless the humouristic intent is highlighted through the symbolism that will be picked up. Therefore, if Freudian slips and jokes contain symbol words, they will be discovered.

Metaphors

A *metaphor* is a literary device designed to assign meaning to a situation or object by drawing a comparison or association to something generally completely unrelated to the dictionary meaning of what is being described. The word *metaphor* stems from the Greek *metaphorá*, translating as "transfer" or "carry over."[13] Through shared reference the non-literal meaning of the metaphor is understood by the general public.[12] Examples include the following:

- A heart of gold is a metaphor for a kind personality.
- A broken heart is a metaphor indicating a person is grieving.

In these examples, *heart* serves as a metaphor for feelings or personality and *broken* and *gold* describe character or mood. More examples include the following:

- Life is a journey.
- Time is money.

These examples highlight a source and target format common to metaphors: the source (*journey* and *money*) represents the concept used to describe or resemble, and the target is what is being described and understood through the metaphor (*life* and *time*).

Metaphors seem to be universal and exist in all known languages but are not exclusively used in linguistics. They are found in other forms of communication, for example, in artwork and other graphical representations and in music. Metaphors also exist in extended narrative forms such as anecdotes and parables that provide a broader illustration of the conveyed message.

Metaphors can eventually become so engrained in the language that they become cliché or empty of meaning; for example, the phrase *to grasp a concept* is a metaphor that can no longer be visualised and so from a symbolic point of view, it has become an empty phrase.

In linguistics, metaphors have evolved into a science unto itself; however, for the purpose of capturing symbol words, only some highlights of its features need to be given in this context as the important fact is that the themes of metaphors chosen varies and trends over time and tends to align with the reigning zeitgeists. Our assumption is that the choice of metaphors is governed by the collective unconscious and the symbol words included in the metaphors will point to which archetypes are being activated.

The common themes that metaphors typically consist of include the following:

- The human body (and characteristics)
- Health and illness
- Animals
- Plants
- Buildings and construction
- Machines and tools
- Games and sports
- Money and economic transactions
- Heat and cold
- Light and darkness
- Forces
- Movement and direction[14]

When comparing the categorisation of archetypes and symbols with the typical metaphor themes, it is worth noting that there are quite a few concurring groupings, something which greatly facilitates the harmonisation of metaphors with archetypes and symbols. However, whether this is only a random phenomena or yet another archetypal structure is something Jung never commented upon; that is, he never pointed to any apparent connections between the two.

Metaphors are usually applied to describe the following targets:

- Emotions
- Desire
- Morality
- Thought
- Society/nation
- Economy
- Human relationship
- Communication
- Time
- Life and death
- Religion
- Events and actions[15]

As highlighted in this list, metaphors usually go from *concrete* to *abstract*, describing mental states, groups and processes, and personal experiences, using tangibles to describe intangibles.

Idioms, or expressions with figurative meaning—in essence any grouping of words whose meaning becomes different from that of each word looked at individually—will provide the most fertile ground in finding symbolism that applies to archetypes. Idioms not only include metaphors but also proverbs, parables, and analogies; they are a common linguistic tool to describe matters and exist in all languages. The English language alone contains at least 25,000 idiomatic expressions.[16]

However, only some of these idioms can be included, because many that contain figurative expressions do not contain archetype-related symbols. Examples of such idioms would include: not having a clue, not standing a chance, reading between the lines, easier said than done, and make my day. In contrast, idioms including archetype-related symbol words include: it makes my blood boil, calm before the storm, the early bird catches the worm, if looks could kill, and red tape.

It is not the figurative meaning of these idioms but the actual use of symbol words in a figurative context, such as the words *blood, storm, catches, kill,* and *red,* that indicates archetypal symbolism and are thus included in the count.

Once the symbolic words or expressions have been documented and registered, they are applied as pick-up filters from regular reviews of media databases to determine if the occurrences of figurative language is increasing or decreasing over time and what themes are currently in vogue.

Some psychologists have compared the use of figurative speech with the structure of the unconscious. The French psychoanalyst Jacques Lacan (1901–1981) claimed that the unconscious follows the structure of a language and borrowed the linguistic concepts of metaphor and metonymy; another figure of speech where an item is not called by its own name but by something closely linked, like using the metonymy *Wall Street* when referring to the financial industry. Lacan argued that the function of the metaphor was to suppress, while the function of metonymy is to combine. Thus, he linked the use of metaphors with the *condensation* defense mechanism; the combination of two symbols into one and metonymy with the *displacement* defense mechanism, which aims to redirect one's focus from something considered socially unacceptable to something acceptable.[17]

Myths, Legends, and Sagas

Myths, legends, and sagas often provide narratives as underlining models for human behaviour. They seem to exist among all cultures and throughout history and many of them share similarities consisting of recurring elements such as archetypal characters, objects, or events that provide (moral) guidance to their audience. Jung used these elements to identify many of the archetypes and references to myths and their content is still a common method to provide references and contexts. In addition to flagging the presence of an activated archetype in the collective unconscious, the emergence of a certain myth, legend, or saga in the public domain will also provide a proposition for the handling of specific situations that the existing conscious mind has difficulty in approaching from a psychological perspective. Myths, therefore, will activate as part of a new zeitgeist that provides a narrative to better deal with reality. The study of myths and observation of their appearance in clustered themes will therefore add useful information of prospective future collective behaviour, and from a measurement purpose, their symbolic contents can be recorded. The number of myths will, like archetypes, be of a finite number, although they come in a great number of variations, which makes their classification cumbersome. As the core elements of myths consist of archetypes, whether in the form of characters, objects, or events, establishing that a myth has become active in the psychological environment will provide guidance of the sequence and timings in which individual archetypes might play out.

In philosophy and sociology, the concept of narratives, referred to as *discourse*, has been extensively researched and has come to mean what can or cannot be debated in the public forum during a specific time epoch. The French philosopher Michel Foucault (1926–1984) highlighted the concept of discourse,[18] pointing out that discourse determines what is considered contemporary dogma and statements to which individuals and society at large need to relate and if challenged by anyone comes with the risk of social outcast. How these discourses appear in the first place is never firmly established by their proponents. No links in these academic fields have so far been made between limiting perception of reality through discourse to archetypal thought patterns in the collective unconscious. The main view is that they can be willfully constructed, as Foucault proposed, and that the discourse is set by those currently in power as a controlling instrument. Another view is that they just appear spontaneously.

A somewhat similar concept in behavioural economics, labeled as *framing*, has been demonstrated by the Israeli economists and Nobel laureates Amos Tversky (1937–1996) and Daniel Kahneman (b. 1934).[19] Through experiments, they showed that the way a problem is being framed and presented can affect what decision is made and it can distort assumed rationality and be used to game and manipulate behaviour and outcomes in a desired way.

Broadly speaking, there are shared functionalities between discourse and framing, with myths supporting the zeitgeists' narratives by constraining the way reality is being perceived and by steering behaviour towards certain paths. But where discourse and framing are claimed to be deliberately provoked, the initiation of myths and archetypes are, according to Jungian theory, autonomous.

Taboos

Taboos are defined as items relating to human activities that are prohibited or strongly condemned based on reigning societal and/or moral and religious convictions.[20] Taboos can also be established on an individual basis and this is how Jung first came to identify personal complexes—the notably strong emotional reaction to a particular word triggering a psychological reaction. An example is the swift change of subject or other typical displacement activities that signal a disturbance in response to the taboo word.

What is or is not considered taboo changes over time and will differ depending on cultural contexts; there seem to be very few items that are perpetually seen as taboo or at least the scope of a certain taboo can vary widely. The incest taboo is defined differently in different parts of the world, with marriages between closely related cousins not being uncommon in certain Middle Eastern cultures. In the interpretations of some religions, the pedophilia taboo is circumvented through child marriages. The cannibalism taboo, at least in its symbolic form, is disregarded as part of the Christian practice of Communion.

Taboos also cover discussion topics, generally seen as issues considered inappropriate by political correctness or the reigning zeitgeist. Also in the financial world, once certain beliefs or opinions take a dogmatic nature any opposing view is considered taboo and consequently is ignored or ridiculed. At the height of a financial bubble, the belief that US property prices could never decline—a view at the time shared publicly by industry leaders, rating agencies, regulators, and politicians—was held to the point that it formed a fundamental condition for business models and policies.

Words representing these taboos are usually replaced with figurative language, particularly euphemisms. Instead of *laying off staff*, the term *rightsizing* is used as an euphemism; *collateral damage* comes to describe *civilians killed during war*. From the perspective of the collective unconscious, understanding the taboos in force helps to provide insights into the shadow aspects, associated projections, and scapegoats and indicates the contents of the archetypes that might come to activate, in an effort to reestablish a holistic balance of the mind. Eventually, these taboos are toned down and drawn back into the public domain as acceptable topics. A historical study of different taboos during different zeitgeists and cultures will clearly note the shifts over time, such as the taboo topic of sexuality in the Victorian era, which is no longer considered taboo in the Western context at least. So it is a worthwhile exercise to record the contemporary taboos and how they are symbolically described, and to monitor the shifting trends and frequency in public appearances as a way to understand the boundaries of the zeitgeist.

Conclusion

That metaphors influence the way we think and can be used to influence decision making and reasoning has been subject to comprehensive studies. For instance, describing crime in terms of *crime epidemics* or *crime waves plaguing a city* leads to a different set of framing and addressing social problems than if crime were described in terms such as a *beast*, or criminals *preying* on victims. These conscious shifts in metaphor themes bring with them changes in policies to fight crime.[21]

The American academics George P. Lakoff and Mark L. Johnson, who have spent a large part of their careers studying metaphors and have published some of the leading work in the area, are proponents of the view that metaphors and symbolic language holds the power to influence not only thought patterns but also actions. Applying war-like, aggressive metaphors to describe matters will influence the thinking in terms of war-like thought structures—*kill his argument, the proposal got slashed*—and leads to more aggressive behaviour.[22] Similar findings have been detected when applying different metaphor types in describing concepts such as time and emotions. The metaphor themes chosen seem to influence reasoning and can therefore lead to different decision outcomes. In general, the influence of metaphors in steering agendas and decision making are not consciously recognised but operate partly unconsciously.[23] Brain scans by functional magnetic resonance imaging (fMRI) suggest that when test subjects read metaphors that reference a particular smell, it not only activates the areas of the brain that interpret written words but also activates those areas in the brain that deal with smell. Therefore, the research highlights that a metaphor can activate additional areas in the brain that triggers a different perception of reality.[24]

The framing of political agendas is a well-known strategy to influence voters and the role that figurative language can play in affecting the outcome of choices, overriding the expected rational choice, is widely used by politicians and advertisers to game the decision-making process. However, it is obvious that not all efforts in framing political debates or advertising campaigns have been successful; using metaphors and similar figurative language sticks in people's minds only when aligned with the reigning zeitgeists. This is what existing research fails to explain: Why do certain metaphor themes become popular at certain times and at other times will not work at all, despite extensive advertising campaigns to popularise concepts, products, or political agendas?

Notes

1. "Active Imagination," Washington Society for Jungian Psychology, www.jung.org/Staples.html (accessed November 30, 2013).
2. "Dreams," in *Jung Lexicon: A Primer of Terms & Concepts*, ed. Daryl Sharp, www.psychceu.com/jung/sharplexicon.html (accessed November 30, 2013).
3. C. G., *On the Nature of Dreams* (Vol. 8 in *The Collected Works of C.G. Jung*), ed. R. F. C. Hull, 2nd ed. (Princeton, NJ: Princeton University Press, 1981), par. 545.
4. Ibid., par. 546.
5. "Intuition," *Oxford English Dictionary*, www.oed.com/ (accessed November 30, 2013).
6. Ibid.
7. C. G. Jung, *Definitions* (Vol. 6 in *The Collected Works of C. G. Jung*), ed. R. F. C. Hull, 2nd ed. (Princeton, NJ: Princeton University Press, 1981), par. 770.

8. "Right-Brain Hemisphere," http://psychology.jrank.org (accessed November 30, 2013).
9. Sigmund Freud, *Psychopathology of Everyday Life* (Radford, VA: Wilder Publications, 2010).
10. Ibid.
11. Ibid.
12. G. P. Lakoff and M. L. Johnson, *Metaphors We Live By*, 2nd ed. (Chicago: University of Chicago Press, 2003).
13. "μεταφορά," in *A Greek–English Lexicon*, ed. Henry George Liddell and Robert Scott, Perseus, www.perseus.tufts.edu/hopper/ (accessed November 30, 2013).
14. Z. Kovecses, *Metaphor: A Practical Introduction*, 2nd ed., chap. 7 (New York: Oxford University Press, 2010).
15. Ibid.
16. R. Jackendoff, *The Architecture of the Language Faculty* (Cambridge, MA: MIT Press, 1997).
17. J. Lacan, "The Instance of the Letter in the Unconscious or Reason Since Freud," chap. 20 in *Ecrits: The First Complete Edition in English*, trans. B. Fink (New York: W.W. Norton & Company, 2007).
18. M. Foucault, *The Archaeology of Knowledge*, reprint ed. (New York: Vintage, 1982).
19. Tversky, *Choices, Values and Frames* (New York: Cambridge University Press, 2000).
20. "Taboo," Encyclopædia Britannica, 2012 (accessed November 30, 2013).
21. P. H. Thibodeau and L. Boroditsky, "Metaphors We Think With: The Role of Metaphor in Reasoning," *PLoS ONE* 6, no. 2 (2011): e16782, www.plosone.org/article/info%3Adoi%2F10.1371%2Fjournal.pone.0016782 (accessed November 30, 2013).
22. Lakoff and Johnson, *Metaphors We Live By*.
23. Thibodeau and Boroditsky, "Metaphors We Think With."
24. A. Murphy Paul, "Your Brain on Fiction," *New York Times*, Sunday Review, March 17, 2012, www.nytimes.com/2012/03/18/opinion/sunday/the-neuro-science-of-your-brain-on-fiction.html?pagewanted=all&_r=0 (accessed November 30, 2013).

References

"Active Imagination." Washington Society for Jungian Psychology. www.jung.org/Staples.html.
Encyclopædia Britannica. 2012. www.britannica.com/ (accessed November 30, 2013).
Foucault, M. 1982. *The Archaeology of Knowledge*. Reprint ed. New York: Vintage.
Freud, S. 2010. *Psychopathology of Everyday Life*. Radford, VA: Wilder Publications.
Jackendoff, R. 1997. *The Architecture of the Language Faculty*. Cambridge, MA: MIT Press.
Jung, C. G. 1981. *The Collected Works of C. G. Jung Vol. 8*. 2nd ed. Princeton, NJ: Princeton University Press.

Kahneman, D., and A. Tversky. 2000. *Choices, Values and Frames*. Cambridge, UK: Cambridge University Press.

Kovecses, Z. 2010. *Metaphor: A Practical Introduction*. 2nd ed. New York: Oxford University Press.

Lacan, J. 2007. *Ecrits: The First Complete Edition in English*. Translated by B. Fink. New York: W.W. Norton & Company.

Lakoff, G. P., and M. L. Johnson. 2003. *Metaphors We Live By*. 2nd ed. Chicago: University of Chicago Press.

Liddell, Henry George, and Robert Scott, eds., "μεταφορά." In *A Greek–English Lexicon*. Perseus, *Oxford English Dictionary*, www.oed.com/ (accessed November 30, 2013).

Paul, A. Murphy. 2012. "Your Brain on Fiction." *New York Times*. Sunday Review, March 17. www.nytimes.com/2012/03/18/opinion/sunday/the-neuroscience-of-your-brain-on-fiction .html?pagewanted=all&_r=0 (accessed November 30, 2013).

"Right-Brain Hemisphere." http://psychology.jrank.org (accessed November 30, 2013).

Sharp, Daryl (ed.). 1991. *Jung Lexicon: A Primer of Terms & Concepts*. www.psychceu.com/ jung/sharplexicon.html.

Thibodeau, P. H., and L. Boroditsky. 2011. "Metaphors We Think With: The Role of Metaphor in Reasoning." *PLoS ONE* 6(2): e16782. www.plosone.org/article/info%3Adoi% 2F10.1371%2Fjournal.pone.0016782. www.perseus.tufts.edu/hopper/ (accessed November 30, 2013).

CHAPTER 7

Developing a Conceptual Measurement Methodology Based on Archetypal Forces

Part II: The Data

Symbols will appear in various forums. However, to achieve an empirically verifiable set of symbols that can be used for measurement purposes, the collation must as far as possible be subject to objective selection criteria and that puts constraints on suitable sources from a data-gathering point of view. Therefore, symbols represented as figurative language, such as metaphors, proverbs, or myths, in text format represent the preferred alternative as the data-gathering efforts can be independently verified and replicated through a set of objective rules.

In the 1920s and 1930s, during Carl Jung's time, a collation effort from a large number of multifaceted media sources would have been enclosed with considerable practical difficulties to manually extract, categorise, and combine the occurrence of symbol words as a time series. Jung and his contemporaries were therefore confined to individual patient analysis and from their consolidated results, they drew conclusions about relationships between behaviour, symbols, and archetypes. Today, however, the extraction and categorisation of data from disparate media sources poses less of a challenge and will provide a better reflection of the inclinations of the collective unconscious than the intrinsically subjective efforts of assessing and categorising individuals' dreams.

The selection of data sources is critical to ensure an all-inclusive reflection of the collective conscious and unconscious. As the priority of empirically testing the methodology is on linking archetypes to globally related financial assets with a tilt towards the US market, the data sources deployed need to cover the larger part of the English-speaking media worldwide. The English-only focus is pivotal because blending different languages would prove problematic. Symbolism varies across languages and cultures, which can represent different zeitgeists. Our focus is on the predominant archetypal forces in the English language and cultural setting. A very symbol-rich language and culture, such as the Chinese, would require its own separate exercise to map symbols and figurative languages to archetypes, universal in structure, but with Chinese characters and a very specific symbolism.

This obviously is a limitation as trends in major financial assets are not exclusively driven from a population that operates and is influenced by an (American) English language and cultural setting. However, a focus on the English-speaking media will provide a proxy reflection of the collective investor sentiments, even if some of these are not likely to belong to the English-speaking sphere. They are still prone to absorb clues from that cultural context, and as such the error with not including other zeitgeist influenced cultures becomes limited, albeit recognised.

Also, given the universal collective unconscious, data pulling points should not be limited to sections of financial news and political broadcasts. Instead, they should cover all types of general news, including culture, defined in its broadest sense; sports and societal events as symbol expressions should occur in all different genre and media, although maybe not evenly. The more dispersed the media areas that symbols can be drawn from, the higher the likelihood that they represent the collective unconscious rather than various individuals' personal conscious attitudes.

Data Sources

When selecting data sources for symbol collation, the following criteria need to be considered:

- Focus on the English-speaking media; however, not exclusively from English-speaking countries.
- Incorporate national, regional, and global coverage.

- Political views of the publication or authors do not matter as the archetypal influence spans over political divergence. Archetypes deal with thought patterns that under activation are not constrained by political views whether left, right, or center. Instead, it is the context within which divergent views operate that will be affected by the archetypes, although to a different degree depending on ideology. Archetypal activity might lead to polarisation in terms of political views; however, it is not the political directions per se that are dictated by the archetypes. For example, a more authoritarian view can be represented both through Communism and Fascism; authoritarianism is the underlying sentiment. In the financial markets, though, the trend shows only one direction, and not all assets will trend in the same direction simultaneously.

- Generally the sources are not broken down by subject, given that doing so is unimportant from the point of view of the collective unconscious, but the development of a time series is done through a consolidated collation, not segregating or weighting included media sources differently. However, at the outburst of a particular symbol theme, it is tracked back to explore the origin of source and subject to determine if it is possible to establish any early warning system indicator and focus the scope of the analytics.

- It covers areas beyond finance and politics; broadly any topic that could be addressed using figurative language, in particular colloquial contents of culture, fashion, fiction, and sports articles but as a rule not technical or scientific documents as these rarely are described through figurative language. The actual articles are in themselves generally not of interest but through the symbols captured, we are interested in what tone the news is presented or described in, determining what type of thematic metaphorical language is being used. This is a fact long noted by media researchers: that a review of news will provide more than just the facts of the specific tenets it aims to describe. The way the news is framed provides insight into the reigning zeitgeists.[1]

- The media coverage is generally article-based but will include transcription of interviews and speeches. Periodicals and books are not included in the database searches. While this may pose a limitation in scope, the particular symbol words in fashion are assumed not to be included only in literature but instead to permeate all written communication and public types of broadcasts. Hence, not being able to include these genres should not distort the analysis.

- With regards to double counting, if articles or part of articles are replicated or quoted, these will be counted as many times as occurring, to gain an understanding of each article's popularity. As part of this framework, circulation or hits per article are not calculated and used to adjust for frequency, as there are technical issues in ensuring comprehensive access to obtaining hits for all articles included in the media sources and cannot be consolidated with circulation numbers of the articles in paper form.

Capture and Cleansing

Once the data sources containing news media have been identified and prepared for extraction of symbol words, capturing and cleansing procedures needs to be established to facilitate the development of a time series used for statistical testing. There are four major steps involved:

1. Apply the symbol dictionary to the data sources and ensure that filters are employed so only words or phrases used in symbolic form are captured, and excluded when used in their literal meaning.
2. Categorise the captured words by archetypal theme and grammatical function.
3. Relativise the symbol words through assessing their frequency versus the total text mass and highlight their relative, rather than absolute, magnitude as the text volumes vary over time, which will distort the trend if using an absolute measurement approach.
4. Conduct an in-depth review if any spikes are detected in the times series versus set thresholds, to investigate the reason for the spike. Why the sudden drastic increase in use of these symbol words? If the investigation points to the inclusion of erroneously labeled figurative language not filtered out by existing rules, then write off the findings. This will facilitate calibration of exclusion filters. If the spike is "legitimate," conduct a review to determine the origins of the spike, in terms of source, topic, and geographics, with a view to establishing early warning indicators.

Capturing of Symbol Words

The capturing of symbols (see Figure 7.1) is based on a weekly extraction from the selected data sources. A symbol word dictionary and context filters are applied to the datafeed. The symbol dictionary consists of a mapping of symbol words and phrases linked to the various archetypes, which are in addition defined by their grammatical attributes, such as subject, object, verb, and adjective. The symbols can consist of single words such as The Warrior or The Mother as subjects, Sun and Apple as objects, verbs such as Massacred and Give Birth, and adjectives like Red or Wise. These can be part of phrases included in proverbs and metaphors, with their synonyms added to the dictionary.

FIGURE 7.1   Weekly Data Extraction

The figure depicts the capturing, cleansing, and categorisation procedures of symbol words from raw text masses into archetype-related time series.

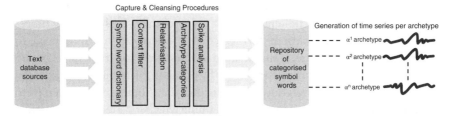

A weekly routine paired with a quarterly review to scan for any new symbol words to be included in the symbol dictionary and mapped to specific archetypes, less important for symbol words that become obsolete as they tend to naturally fall out of the current vocabulary.

An analysis based on the particular word's position in a sentence will help determine its grammatical attribute; for instance, the word *birth* with a preceding *the* or *give* will determine whether it is classified as an object or verb. More crude rules of thumb will assist in the classification, such as a verb follows a subject rather than an object. In all, the symbol word dictionary counts the number of idiomatic phrases and single words and associated synonyms in its thousands. Important to note, especially for individual symbol words, is that no matter the number of rules introduced to segregate them from the non-symbolic population, there will be a number of boundary issues that rudimentary semantic rules and algorithms are not able to pick up. Therefore, the capturing model for single symbol words comes with a certain lack of precision. This requires manual review of each recorded spike to determine validity. However, regarding phrases of figurative language, the extraction from the data sources becomes less of a challenge as the search string can clearly define the combination of words that manifests them as symbolic, like "heart of gold" and "fight fire with fire," obviously omitting in these examples the prepositions *of* and *with* as well as all cases of conjunctions and determiners since they bear no reference to archetypes. The number of occurrences where such specific text strings do not appear as figurative language are relatively rare.

When increases of a symbol word become clearly marked as a spike on a chart, exceeding preset thresholds to distinguish it from "normal" levels of fluctuation, this requires an analysis to look for matching spike patterns symbol words sharing the same theme. The design of the model is such that a spike in a single symbol word alone is not sufficient to trigger a signal of an archetypal activity. There needs to be evidence that a plethora of symbol words within the same thematic cluster indicates increasing frequency. To understand the origin of the spikes and their validity, a review mechanism is applied at the most atomic level, article by article, to help confirm whether the existing filters truly excluded words used literally and not symbolically. This cleansing procedure is logged to establish if further context filters can be introduced to strengthen the procedure. This desktop investigation for each spike is also conducted to detect the underlying driver by pinning down sources of origin, by topic, geography, and even down to individual contributors, as an attempt to identify early warning indicators and determine whether patterns in those areas exist. It will also provide insight into whether the collective unconscious can be consciously manipulated or at least the specific contents of an archetypal trend can be influenced. To qualify as spike, the increase needs to last over several consecutive weeks in order to reduce the probability of including random outbursts just occurring in a single week.

The symbol dictionary needs to be updated on a regular basis to include new synonyms or idioms because language is a living organism in which new words are created while other words become obsolete; at times a specific word can take a different connotation, but rarely in its symbolic meaning. As the measurement model is not based on the individual word but through a set a thematic words required to increase in parallel to trigger a signal, that construction makes the model robust enough not to be influenced by such individual changes in the population of figurative language. The representation of archetypes stays broadly the same over time. Of course 100 years ago no one would use a metaphor such "the big bazooka" to describe expansive monetary policy; now its symbolic meaning is well understood among contemporaries. But when an archetype activates, it will be through a plethora of symbol words, like an uptrend in the symbolic meaning of the word *bazooka* in isolation need not point to the awakening of a war and potential phallic-related archetypes; rather, it needs to be verified through the sudden increase of related words. However, as the data analysis for this exercise does not stretch over a century nor over multiple decades, the potential migration in the symbolic meaning of words becomes less of an issue.

In addition to the weekly capturing and collation routines paired with ad-hoc reviews of any recorded spikes, a quarterly review to scan for any new symbol words to be included in the symbol dictionary and mapped to specific archetypes is included to ensure comprehensive capture of the most recent symbolism and to minimise false signals. However, it is less important for symbol words that become obsolete as they tend to naturally fall out of the current vocabulary.

Hence, in drawing out symbol words from text masses, traditional text mining and analysis are in general less applicable because the key distinction of this measurement methodology is being able to differentiate between the symbolic and literal meaning of words and phrases. Nevertheless, certain text mining techniques are valuable to incorporate as part of the cleansing procedures, such as establishing the grammatical function of a word through its position in a sentence. Others such as name entity recognition, applying disambiguation, and the use of contextual clues (to distinguish where, for example, Moon refers to the symbolic mean of moon and neither the physical satellite nor the UN secretary-general Ban Ki-moon. In this particular case, context filters need to be set up for the single symbol word *Moon*, so it is not included when appearing in the same text as the United Nations (or UN) or in the same context as space or planetary topics in its literal form. However, when the word appears in its symbolic form, such as "moon struck" or "man in the moon," it is picked up. Similar is true for the word *Apple*; appearances related to the corporation and its products as well as the fruit need to be filtered out but in its symbolic form, such as "a few bad apples" or "the apple of my eye," even if included in an article about Apple Inc., would be counted. Such context filters need to be applied in a bespoke manner to each individual symbol word to ensure that the time series includes only occurrences where the words are applied in their symbolic theme. Even if establishing all-encompassing filters is hard to achieve, their calibration is facilitated through spike analysis to determine if the filters have not been rigidly enough applied and the selection has been contaminated.

Cleansing of Symbol Words

A number of filters need to be introduced to facilitate the cleansing and to ensure the true population of symbol words among the media sources, all sharing the objective to emphasise how archetypes colour the thinking and the context which helps frame human decision making.

To start with, the conscious political sentiment of a particular author is of no importance; for or against a certain political topic, being a conservative or socialist need not be considered as part of the symbol review. Being able to exclude such concerns helps to simplify the cleansing procedure and analysis, something which traditional sentiment analysis struggles with as it needs to consider the contextual polarity. Adjusting for ironic statements and linguistic nuances needs to be factored into the model to be able to capture the emotional state of the author. Incorporating these factors becomes a challenge for sentiment analysis algorithms and determining the actual underlying sentiment of the text becomes difficult. This highlights the difference between text analysis and symbol analysis as it does not really matter whether the symbols are used in a positive or negative connotation, in an ironic fashion or not; what matters is the fact they are being used and how often, which demonstrates their importance in influencing perceptions.

Once the cleansing is completed and only the symbol words remain, with everything else removed and stripped out, what should emerge is overarching news, topic, political view, or geographical location, on the aggregate level, so the symbols then become clearly visible, revealing the language of the collective unconscious. Through the accumulated approach, any material from individuals' personal unconscious is reduced to noise, with all unnecessary contents excluded, leaving only the figurative language to focus on, revealing what archetypal thought patterns govern the mind. It is only through the consolidated study of all-encompassing media sources that hidden patterns of archetypal activities will appear in the text layers and this generally represents only a portion of the total text mass. At first, authors and audience are consciously unaware of the unconscious archetypal thought patterns they are communicating and receiving through the symbols, which reinforces the archetypal power. Eventually it enters the conscious, the symbols become fads and fashions, and their frequency increases exponentially and starts to influence behaviour and decision making on a collective scale.

In addition to using contextual filters to help rule out the literal meaning of words according to their symbolism or the symbol dictionary definition, there are a number of other rules that help in the cleansing of symbol words:

- It does not matter in what tense the figurative language is being presented: past, present, or future. It is the time stamp of the article or news piece that matters and dictates to what date in the time series the occurrence of the symbol word is pinned, even if the particular section including the symbolic language related to a previous quotation. The unconscious does not distinguish between tenses.[2]
- Ignore whether a symbolic word is preceded by a negative or presented in an ironic manner reversing its meaning. This does not cancel out or revert its influence; studies in hypnotic technique have demonstrated that the unconscious does not consider negations.[3] The important thing is that the particular symbol words are being used, even if their meaning is reversed.
- Do not differentiate whether the symbolic language is being used to advocate for or against a particular topic. Again, it is the actual increased use of a theme of symbols that highlights what kind of thought patterns are dominating the debate and what type of outcomes are likely, whether financial, political, or social.

- Count repetitions of symbols in the same text. If they occur as referrals or quotations from article to article, this gives an indication of the symbols' popularity.
- Ignore whether the symbol words appear as singular or plural occurrences. They should be counted per appearance in the text; although noted is that certain numerals in themselves are archetypes.
- Only analyse the topic from the perspective of tracking down the origins to the spike for the specific theme of symbol words and identify early adopters of unconscious thought; for instance, whether mainly appearing in the sports section or distinct cultural manifestations, noting the type of publication and the geographics. For the purpose of developing the time series, these are consolidated at an aggregated level and not per topic, source, or geography.

So in essence, once the true symbol words have been extracted and isolated, the review helps draw out the underlying archetypes that are lurking in the text and eventually the connections become visible. It then comes down to studying their frequencies over time and how they correlate to asset prices. No deeper analysis is required, which therefore means a large degree of the work can be automated and so help minimise the manual steps and circumvent any of the subjective scoring required in traditional text sentiment analysis.

Relativisation of Symbol Words

As the text volumes included in the media sources will vary over time, taking an absolute count approach of the symbol words risks distortion. That is, its volumes can go up as the total volume of text increases but that really will not convey its relative importance if the increase is not equal percentage-wise. Therefore, the number of symbol words counted on a weekly basis needs to be relativised with the total number of words included in the media sources. As a matter of simplification, linked references in online articles are not included, as they might or might not contain symbol words; if they do not appear in the included articles of that particular week, they will not be counted. The symbol words' relative popularity is not assessed on an article-by-article basis only counting those which contain symbol words, but rather on the total number of words that constitutes the included articles of the particular week, whether actually including symbol words or not.

To understand the popularity of each article, ideally its circulation, in online media measured through the number of views included, this should also incorporate previously published articles viewed under that week. However, due to technical difficulties with consolidating the number of views from dispersed media sources, this approach was not considered for the first generation of the measurement methodology, which would have been a preferred weighting system for the individual articles containing symbol words to help gauge its popularity. So for the current approach, a crude assumption is that the public acceptance of symbolic themes can be sufficiently assessed through their appearance in the number of articles.

Two Article Examples

The selection, classification, and relativisation of symbol words is demonstrated through the sampling of a couple of articles.[4]

The actual symbol words per article are generally very few, normally never over a couple of percentage points, so taking the big data approach becomes critical in drawing emerging patterns of symbolic language. Words with symbolic meaning are highlighted in **bold**.

World Keeps Full Faith in U.S. Treasuries If Not Politics
By Simon Kennedy, Aki Ito & Alaa Shahine—Oct 14, 2013 4:34 AM GMT+0800

Finance chiefs from nations holding more than $1.3 trillion of Treasuries signaled no plans to sell even as the U.S. **faced** condemnation for the fiscal fight **plaguing** the world's largest economy.

Policy makers from Japan, India, Russia and Saudi Arabia expressed faith in the ability of the U.S. to pay its bills as the potential for default dominated the annual meetings of the International Monetary Fund and World Bank, which ended yesterday in Washington.

With the government now partly closed for almost two weeks and an Oct. 17 **deadline** looming for a boost to its borrowing authority, the U.S. found itself in the rare position of being **blasted** for its economic policy making by foreign officials more used to being the subject of its ire.

"There's no other way than for the U.S. government itself and the U.S. Congress to sort it out," Japanese Finance Minister Taro Aso told Bloomberg Television's Sara Eisen. Fahad Almubarak, chief of Saudi Arabia's central bank, told reporters that "the U.S. current crisis will go away and we think its effect won't be lasting on our investments."

The combination of criticism and confidence was echoed by Pacific Investment Management Co.'s Chief Executive Officer Mohamed El-Erian, who said the manager of the world's biggest bond fund is still holding short-term Treasuries in anticipation of lawmakers increasing the $16.7 trillion U.S. debt ceiling.

"When push comes to **shove** there will be an agreement," El-Erian told a financial industry conference on the sidelines of the IMF meeting. A default would "trigger failures" in collateral markets and "be a **big blow** to the economy," he said.

Yields Rise

Rates on Treasury bills maturing through the end of the year rose last week as lawmakers sought a short-term compromise. Rates on bills due on Nov. 29 climbed 12 basis points, or 0.12 percentage point, to 0.16 percent last week, according to Bloomberg Bond Trader prices. Yields on benchmark Treasury 10-year notes gained four basis points on the week to 2.69 percent.

Treasury Secretary Jacob J. Lew used the presence of foreign counterparts to highlight the risks of inaction, saying the U.S. is the "**anchor** of the international financial system" and its assets enjoy a **haven** status.

"The United States cannot take this hard earned reputation for granted," he told the IMF's steering committee.

That reputation may be intact. While Treasuries have become "mildly less attractive," Reserve Bank of India Governor Raghuram Rajan said "we are not selling our U.S. assets, we are holding on to them." Almubarak of Saudi Arabia, the world's largest oil exporter, said "we are long-term investors" and "our long-term view is positive."

Long-term Investment

"Our investment in U.S. Treasuries is a long-term investment so I don't think there's any major need for major revisions to how our reserves are invested," Russian Finance Minister Anton Siluanov told reporters. "What's happening today, I hope, is a fairly short-term situation."

As of the end of July, Japan held $1.14 trillion of Treasuries, second only to China's $1.28 trillion, according to U.S. Treasury Department data. Russia had $132 billion and India $59 billion.

Attention shifted to Senate leaders yesterday to find a deal that averts a default and restores full government operations. Earlier, Senate Democrats rejected a proposal from Senator Susan Collins, a Maine Republican, saying the debt-limit increase in her plan, to January, was too short to provide certainty, and the funding extension at Republican-preferred levels, until March, was too long.

Rare Position

With the government now partly closed for almost two weeks and an Oct. 17 deadline looming for a boost to its borrowing authority, the U.S. found itself in the rare position of being **blasted** for its economic policy making by foreign officials more used to being the subject of its ire.

Just two years ago, then-U.S. Treasury Secretary Timothy F. Geithner used the gathering of global policy makers to warn Europe that failure to resolve its debt crisis risked "" **cascading** default, bank **runs** and catastrophic risk." Japan has often been lectured for not **beating** deflation and China for the value of the yuan.

"The **overarching** theme is that all of the finance ministers and central bankers are delighted to have this distraction that everyone's **beating** up on the U.S. and not them," said Harvard University professor Kenneth Rogoff, a former chief economist at the IMF in a Bloomberg Television interview.

"There's no schadenfreude," European Union Economic and Monetary Affairs Commissioner Olli Rehn said in a Bloomberg TV interview. "In Europe we are very concerned."

Urgent Action

The fear, expressed by officials and bankers from around the world, is that failure by U.S. politicians to end their **logjam** would **roil** financial markets and cause recession. That concern was reflected in a call by the Group of 20 leading industrial and emerging economies for the U.S. to take "urgent action to address short-term fiscal uncertainties."

"It's quite obvious that if this situation were to last a long time, this would be negative, very negative for the U.S. economy and the world economy," European Central Bank President Mario Draghi said Oct. 12 in Washington.

Draghi **echoed** others in predicting U.S. delinquency would be dodged because of the economic and financial **havoc** it would **wreak**.

A default "would **ripple** through the global economy in a way you couldn't possibly understand," said JPMorgan Chase & Co. CEO Jamie Dimon. Baudouin Prot, chairman of Paris-based BNP Paribas SA, said the consequences "would be absolutely disastrous, considering the role of the U.S. dollar."

Emerging Markets

The state of emerging markets was the other main subject of debate as German Finance Minister Wolfgang Schaeuble said "risks have shifted" in their direction. The IMF predicts developing nations are on course this year for the weakest growth since 2009, when they helped lift the world from recession.

The worry of such economies is that the Federal Reserve and other major central banks will pull back monetary stimulus too fast, prompting an **exodus** of capital and higher borrowing costs.

"There is transition tension," South Korean Finance Minister Hyun Oh Seok said in an interview. The risk of a backlash means policies need to be managed "cautiously," he said.

Emerging markets were in turn told to fortify their own economies, especially those with current account deficits. The Fed's September decision to delay a tapering of its $85 billion asset-purchase program was viewed as buying more time for countries to act.

"**Spillovers** should not be an excuse for emerging economies not doing what many of them need to do," said U.K. Chancellor of the Exchequer George Osborne.

Mexico central bank Governor Agustin Carstens said if the Fed was responding to a strengthening of expansion that may ultimately be the best news.

"If the Fed manages to get a strong U.S. economy, that will benefit all the world," he said in an interview.

Statistics over Symbol Appearances

Number of extracted symbols out of the article: 23	
Article—total number of words: 1,158	
Root symbols, the direct representations of a particular archetype	**dead** line **exodus**
Auxiliary subjects	none
Auxiliary objects	**anchor** **haven** **logjam** **Spillovers** big **blow**
Auxiliary verbs	**faced** **plaguing** **blasted** (two occurrences) **shove** **cascading** **runs** **beating** (two occurrences) **roil** **echoed** **wreak . . . havoc** **ripple**
Auxiliary adjectives	**overarching** **big** blow
Thematic clusters	Death related; **dead** line **wreak** . . . **havoc** **blow** **Beating, blasted plaguing**
	maritime; **anchor, haven, logjam, spillovers, cascading**

U.S. Risks Joining 1933 Germany in Pantheon of Deadbeat Defaults
By John Glover—Oct 14, 2013 7:01 AM GMT+0800

Reneging on its debt obligations would make the U.S. the first major Western government to default since Nazi Germany 80 years ago.

Germany unilaterally ceased payments on long-term borrowings on May 6, 1933, three months after Adolf Hitler was installed as Chancellor. The default helped cement Hitler's power base following years of political instability as the Weimar Republic struggled with its crushing debts.

"The Fed is not going to taper while the government is shut down," said Dean Maki, chief U.S. economist at Barclays Plc in New York. "One, there is a weight on the economy and, two, the Fed calls itself 'data dependent' and it's hard to be data dependent when there's no data coming out."

"These are generally catastrophic economic events," said Professor Eugene N. White, an economics historian at Rutgers University in New Brunswick, New Jersey. "There is no happy ending."

The debt reparations piled onto Germany, which in 1913 was the world's third-biggest economy, sparked the hyperinflation, borrowings and political deadlock that brought the Nazis to power, and the default. It shows how excessive debt has capricious results, such as the civil war and despotism that ravaged Florence after England's Edward III refused to pay his obligations from the city-state's banks in 1339, and the Revolution of 1789 that followed the French Crown's defaults in 1770 and 1788.

Failure by the world's biggest economy to pay its debt in an interconnected, globalized world risks an array of devastating consequences that could lay waste to stock markets from Brazil to Zurich and bring the $5 trillion market in Treasury-backed loans to a halt. Borrowing costs would soar, the dollar's role as the world's reserve currency would be in doubt and the U.S. and world economies would risk plunging into recession—and potentially depression.

Senate Talks

Senate leaders of both parties are negotiating to avert a U.S. default after a lapse in borrowing authority takes effect Oct. 17, even as senators block legislation to prevent one and talks between the White House and House Republicans have hit an impasse. Democratic lawmakers said Oct. 12 that the lack of movement may have an effect on financial markets. After Oct. 17, the U.S. will have $30 billion plus incoming revenue and would start missing payments sometime between Oct. 22 and Oct. 31, according to the Congressional Budget Office.

Serial Defaulter

Germany, staggering under the weight of 132 billion gold marks in war reparations and not permitted to export to the victors' markets, was a serial defaulter from 1922, according to Albrecht Ritschl, a professor of economic history at the London School of Economics. That forced the country to borrow to pay its creditors, in what Ritschl calls a Ponzi scheme.

"Reparations were at the **heart** of the issue in the interwar years," Ritschl said in a telephone interview. "The big question is why anyone lent a dime to Germany with those hanging over them. The assumption must have been that reparations would eventually go away."

While a delinquent corporation may go out of business, be broken up, sold to a competitor, or otherwise change its shape, sovereign defaulters are different. Weimar Germany deferred payments, stopped transfers, reformed the currency and wrote down debt, wringing a series of agreements from its creditors before the Nazis repudiated the obligations in 1933.

It took until the 1953 London Debt Agreement to **lay to rest** the nation's reparations difficulties, essentially by postponing any payments until after reunification in 1990 of East and West Germany, according to Timothy Guinnane, Professor of Economic History at Yale University in New Haven, Connecticut. The U.S., eager to ensure Germany was a **bulwark** against communism, pressured creditors to agree to debt relief, according to Guinnane.

Economic Strain

"The U.S. was not being generous or magnanimous in the London Debt Agreement, it rarely is," Guinnane said in an e-mail. "Rather, it understood that if Germany was forced to repay all the debts it technically owed, it would put the new Federal Republic under intolerable political and economic strain."

Payments on about 150 million euros ($203 million) of bonds issued to fund reparations ended in October 2003, according to the Associated Press.

After sovereign defaults and before a nation is allowed to borrow again, some sort of repayment is typically made, Carmen Reinhart and Kenneth Rogoff wrote in their 2009 book on sovereign bankruptcies "This Time Is Different." While Russia's Bolshevik government refused to pay Tsarist debts, when the country re-entered debt markets it negotiated a **token** payment on the debt, according to the book.

Germany, France

Germany and France have both defaulted eight times since 1800, according to Reinhart and Rogoff. While Germany was sufficiently big and strategically important to be helped to peaceful prosperity by its creditors, default typically doesn't end well for smaller nations.

Serial defaulters Argentina and Greece have retained political, if not economic independence. The Latin American nation failed to meet its commitments five times since 1951 and in 2001 gained the record for the largest-ever restructuring, a distinction it held until overtaken by

Greece in 2012. Argentina's bondholders are still pursuing the nation through the courts.

Including 2012, Greece has defaulted six times since 1826, three years before it gained independence, and has spent more than half the years since 1800 in default, according to Reinhart and Rogoff.

The biggest emerging-markets defaults in the past 15 years illustrate the cycle of contagion that typically marks sovereign debt crises.

Russian Restructuring

Russia halted payments on $40 billion of local debt in 1998 after oil, its main export, plunged 42 percent amid a global economic slowdown triggered by the Asian financial crisis. By the time it devalued the ruble and defaulted that August, the government had **drained** about half its foreign reserves and made an unsuccessful bid to increase the $22.6 billion international aid package it had received.

Russia's debt restructuring prompted investors to pull out of emerging markets, **plunging** Argentina into recession. By December 2001, when the South American country halted payments on $95 billion of bonds, the economy had contracted three successive years, **cutting** into tax revenue and pushing foreign reserves down to almost a six-year low.

Those defaults took place because events had rendered the nations insolvent, something that doesn't apply to the U.S., said the LSE's Ritschl.

"The only situation that really parallels the U.S. situation at present is the U.S. situation," he said. "There's really no doubt about the solvency of the U.S. Treasury."

Statistics over Symbol Appearances

Number of extracted symbols out of the article: 23	
Article—total number of words: 1,096	
Root symbols, the direct representations of a particular archetype	Pantheon deadbeat deadlock impasse heart bulwark
Auxiliary subjects	none
Auxiliary objects	waste token

Auxiliary verbs	cement crushing taper weight piled sparked lapse block hit lay to rest drained plunging (two occurrences) cutting
Auxiliary adjectives	none
Thematic clusters	death; **cutting hit crushing** **deadbeat deadlock impasse**
	construction; **block piled** **cement bulwark**

The percentage calculation of the number of symbol words versus total text mass is (23 plus 23 equals 47) divided by (1,158 plus 1,096 equals 2,254), which comes to 2.1 percent of the total population, and is a typical percentage of the relation between the representation of symbolic language in the average news article. Generally, there is a slightly higher percentage in articles of a cultural nature. The relative frequency for the individual symbol word is calculated through the number of appearances, such as the single occurrence of *Pantheon*, whose relative frequency for this assumed time interval would be one word divided by 2,254 words or 0.044 percent. This relative frequency is added to the time series for the particular time period and compared to the previous frequency levels to determine whether it should be regarded as noise, or if exceeding a preset threshold, indicates part of a spike. As pointed out, a signal is not triggered through the spike of a single symbol word alone but needs to be among a cluster of symbol words sharing the same characteristics, all spiking in parallel, pointing to a new trend in the symbolic way that reality is being described. In this particular example, there are no related symbol words to *Pantheon* appearing; as such, it is not considered a signal even if in isolation indicating a spike.

From this particular sampling of just two articles, one can note that there is some higher representation of the Death archetype, and the maritime theme and construction theme are used as symbolic language. If these themes also appear in topics other than economy and politics, such as sports and culture, and it constitutes an increasing trend taking in how reality is being described, this could point to the archetype Death in, for example, a maritime context, as emerging. This could lead to metaphors such as "drowning in work" and "bloodbath" becoming common, and through studying past symbol spikes of such archetypes and linking them to moves in particular financial assets, one can then make projections on future price trends.

A context filter would have excluded the word *heart* if it, for instance, had appeared in a medical article and reflected its literal meaning; however, if, as in the sample article, it was included to convey a symbolic meaning, then it would have been counted.

Through a consolidated approach, over time, the levels of noise can be distinguished from spikes, but the threshold needs to be set individually for each symbol word. Generally, however, the spikes are so clearly noticeable that a review of a graphical depiction tends to clearly distinguish them.

Conclusion

Once the building blocks have been clearly defined as demonstrated in Chapter 6, the collation can initiate, and rules for selection need to clearly filter out words used literally versus figuratively to avoid contamination and ending up with a distorted population of words that goes into the development of a time series. Also it is the words' relative rather than absolute occurrences that matter.

Notes

1. G. Gerbner and G. Marvanyi, "The Many Worlds of the World's Press," *Journal of Communication*, 27, no. 1 (1977): 52–75.
2. S. Freud, *The Unconscious* (London: Penguin Modern Classics Translated Texts, 2005).
3. W. S. Kroger and M. D. Yapko, "Introduction," in *Clinical & Experimental Hypnosis: In Medicine, Dentistry, and Psychology*, 2nd rev. ed. with DVD (Philadelphia: Lippincott Williams & Wilkins, 2007), 48.

4. S. Kennedy, A. Ito, and A. Shahine, "World Keeps Full Faith in U.S. Treasuries If Not Politics," Bloomberg.com, October 14, 2013, www.bloomberg.com/news/ 2013–10–13/world-keeps-full-faith-in-u-s-treasuries-if-not-politics.html (accessed November 30, 2013); J. Glover, "U.S. Risks Joining 1933 Germany in Pantheon of Deadbeat Defaults," Bloomberg.com, October 14, 2013, www.bloomberg .com/news/2013–10–13/u-s-risks-joining-1933-germany-in-pantheon-of-deadbeat-defaults.html (accessed November 30, 2013).

References

Freud, S. 2005. *The Unconscious*. London: Penguin Modern Classics Translated Texts.
Gerbner, G., and G. Marvanyi 1977. "The Many Worlds of the World's Press." *Journal of Communication 27*(1): 52–75.
Glover, J. 2013. "U.S. Risks Joining 1933 Germany in Pantheon of Deadbeat Defaults." Bloomberg.com, October 14. www.bloomberg.com/news/2013–10–13/u-s-risks-joining-1933-germany-in-pantheon-of-deadbeat-defaults.html (accessed November 30, 2013).
Kennedy, S., A. Ito, and A. Shahine 2013. "World Keeps Full Faith in U.S. Treasuries If Not Politics." Bloomberg.com. October 14. www.bloomberg.com/news/2013–10–13/world-keeps-full-faith-in-u-s-treasuries-if-not-politics.html (accessed November 30, 2013).
Kroger, W. S., and M.D. Yapko 2007. "Introduction." In *Clinical & Experimental Hypnosis: In Medicine, Dentistry, and Psychology*. 2nd rev. ed. with DVD. Philadelphia: Lippincott Williams & Wilkins.

CHAPTER 8

Developing a Conceptual Measurement Methodology Based on Archetypal Forces

Part III: The Model

When the time series of the symbol counts have been constructed and generated, they can be tested one by one by symbol for leading correlation versus time series of financial assets. However, if correlation is found, it is generally of a partial nature, given that the characteristics of archetypes are singular in direction, like that of risk averse versus risk aggressive, and will subsequently only indicate price movements either up or down and rarely both. This puts constraints on which statistical test methods one can deploy; for example, using R-square values comparing two time series with such different characteristics becomes less suitable as they are not designed to cater to one-sided leading correlations but rank correlation parallel in time and symmetric higher.

Given that the symbol words have been extracted from overwhelmingly (American) English media reflecting that particular culture and psychological environment, testing needs to be aligned with investment alternatives that typically dominate within that sphere. This would include the broader US stock market index, the S&P 500, an associated "fear" index used to gauge appetite for risk, i.e., the VIX, and some specific industrial equity index, which can be *assumed* to be linked to particular archetypes, such as war-related industries, gaming-related industries, and healthcare-related industries. The focus needs to be on indexes rather than individual stocks as they correspond better to the general market view and sentiments and filter out any company-specific idiosyncratic factors that would distort the relationship between the psychological perception of value and fundamental valuation and corporate activities such as mergers and acquisitions.

In addition, some commodities although not exclusively US-related are also included as they traditionally have been linked to archetypal symbols. So prior to the testing, links are made to "natural connections" between certain financial assets and archetypes, such as Earth-related archetypes being linked to Earth-related commodities, Sun to gold, and Moon to silver; likewise, risk aggressive archetypes are linked to high levels in the VIX. These come to serve as the starting point for the testing: to seek leading correlation between the core symbol elements of such archetypes and the associated financial assets. As a prerequisite for continued testing, leading correlations with *high significance* between them need to be proven to merit continued testing between archetypes and financial assets where the relationships are not as obvious.

Once correlations have been established, each case needs to be investigated to determine whether the archetypal signals really are precursors to the actual moves in the asset prices or are merely precursors to another set of recurring drivers that establish price trends, for example, war-oil, inflation-gold, expansive monetary policy and links to asset prices, unemployment, and so on. When possible, this review is done through statistical testing of proxy indicators with the symbol time series and through a desktop review of similar events, such as conflicts or war, that are recurring in time, succeeding spikes for symbols words.

The statistical testing is focused on positive signals only; that is, when a signal in the archetypal symbol words leads to a positive or negative price move in the associated asset, negatives (no signal and no move) with the exception of the VIX, where archetypes with risk averse characteristics will be tested for the absence of spikes in the VIX, would be excluded.

The time duration for the tests starts from the inception of the millennia, based on weekly time units. The constraint of not being able to go further back in time is due to difficulties in getting access to broad enough media coverage for collating symbols. This constitutes a limitation, as a longer duration would have been able to include more financial bubbles and longer-term trends in the financial markets to test against and would have provided more robustness to the testing. However, for this first step, the test period spans from January 2000 to July 2013.

Signal Theory

Through studying the fluctuations in the time series of the various symbol words, some characteristics in their amplitude emerge. Typically they move in tightly ranged patterns, similar to noise, and sudden eruptions of spikes rather than features of longer, slowly increasing uptrends; their return back to the noise pattern is also categorised by a rapid move down rather than a longer declining trend. The shared commonality among these symbol words seems to be that they follow a noise-signal pattern. Applying pattern recognition testing confirms these assumptions. However, the scale of the noise levels and their relative frequency varies greatly, simply meaning that some symbol words are more common in daily vocabulary than others without having triggered a spike, as do the proportions of the spikes and time intervals, as can be noted in Figure 8.1. What is noise and what are spikes can therefore not be established through single relative levels but need to be individually determined, symbol word by symbol word, through the study of historical performance. The noise levels represent the slumbering archetypes with the spikes as their awakening and pushing into the conscious level of the mind, inserting new thought patterns, which with some delay will start to impact behaviour and decision making. The noise-spike pattern that emerges thus corroborates well with the Jungian theories on the binary nature of archetypes as being either dormant or active. Also, there is little evidence of trending in the relativised symbol frequency over time, and a lack of incline or decline in the noise ranges over the testing period; this is a shared characteristic among all tested symbol words.

Given these traits, signal theory becomes one approach to help describe the fluctuations of the symbol words, as it would help distinguish "true" signals from the regular interval of noise and assists to develop a model, which if exceeding a certain threshold, calculated based on the normal range of the noise, is considered a valid signal.

The signal theory was developed in the 1950s using mathematical statistics to help detect signals as part of electronic communication but has since come to be deployed in other areas as well, most recently to determine useful versus irrelevant information in online communication as a way to exclude spam and other items that obstruct communication. To facilitate such assessments, a signal-to-noise ratio is applied to calculate the relationship between true and false information.[1]

One approach to distinguishing between spikes and noise is to study the differing distributions between the noise and the noise plus the spikes. To standardise the review, the assumed distributions hold Gaussian properties,

FIGURE 8.1 A Graphic Representation of the Atypical Signal-Noise Characteristics of Symbol Words

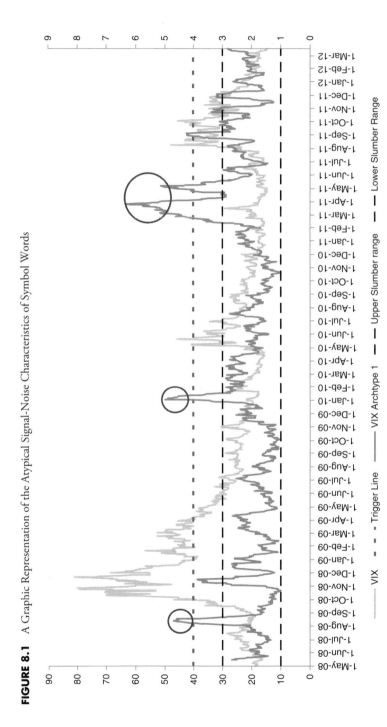

134

FIGURE 8.2 A Distinction between the Noise Distribution and the Noise Plus Spike Distribution, Highlighting the Signal Threshold

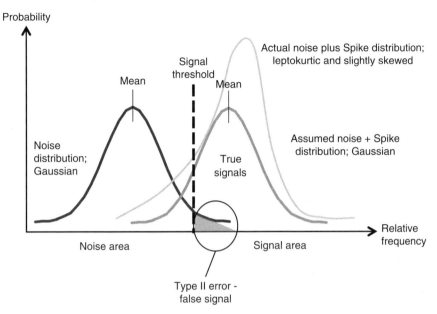

which largely concur with the empirical parameters of the noise distribution but the spikes are more leptokurtic in shape, meaning more extreme in terms of minimums and maximums above the threshold than a Gaussian distribution would suggest. However, for ease of calculation, a Gaussian distribution is applied with the model error acknowledged, although each actual spike signal is in addition graphically observed and reviewed as a mitigant to address potential model errors. Through the study of the fluctuations in the symbol words we noted a generic, across all symbol words, minimum threshold level, set in a *constant relation to the dynamic noise frequency levels* to what constitutes a valid signal as well as what seems to be an upper maximum. However, the variations within the absolute minimums and maximums vary greatly.

When the spike values are added to the noise distribution, the distribution is shifted to the right along the relative frequency axis. To simplify the calculations, both these distributions are normalised with the mean of the noise distribution set to zero and the standard deviations of both distributions assumed to be the value of one. A signal will be noted in accordance with the noise plus spike distribution and if no signal is observed, the weekly values of the symbol words will follow the noise distribution.

Parts of the signals will be false, a Type II error; however, within acceptable ranges, such as false errors not exceeding 10 percent of the total signal population, they will not trigger a calibration of the threshold levels. Type I errors, that is, no signals triggered when an actual financial trend move occurs, are picked up through backtesting (see Figure 8.2).

Correlation Testing

Given the asymmetrical and leading correlation between the time series of the symbol words and the prices of financial assets, statistical testing to quantify the levels of correlation needs to consider the delay factor between the signal and start of the price trend. The testing hypothesis assumes that the time distance between the peak level of the signal and the start of the price trend of the associated financial asset should be a constant, regardless of symbol word or financial asset with the only adjustable of that constant being the intensity and magnitude of the spike above the dynamic threshold that distinguishes spikes from noise. In other words, the greater the magnitude, the shorter should be the distance between the signal spike and start of the price trend (see Figure 8.3).

Assuming an agnostic time constant as a condition for the hypothesis supports the general and universal characteristics of archetypes proposed by

FIGURE 8.3   Signal Peak and Signal Threshold

Through empirical testing, we arrive at a constant for the distance in time between the signal peak and the start of the associated financial assets price trend; the relative intensity of the signal peak serves as an adjustable variable to the time distance constant.

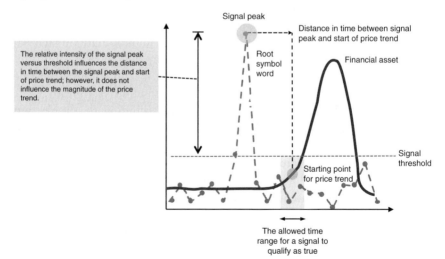

Jung, with a standardised psychological mechanism between the timing of the activation of any archetype until its proactive influence of investment behaviour, regardless of asset and regardless of direction in price trend.

Given the pattern of noise and spikes with little evidence of trending and seasonality in the data, it is not necessary to cleanse the symbol word's time series.

The time distance between the empirical price data and symbol words, adjusted for the intensity in the spikes, provides in accumulation a mean, maximum, and minimum around which the peak signals cluster. Plotting all these time points, the distribution takes a leptokurtic form with a greater number of time points around the mean but with longer tails than a Gaussian distribution would suggest. As part of this graphical review it is important to determine if there are any groupings per themes of symbol words, as that would point to different response times for differing archetypes and thus not support the hypothesis of archetypes as a universal structure.

To facilitate the graphical analysis, cross correlations were used to determine the location in time, with the empirically determined mean serving as a starting point to initiate the formal testing. The testing is simplified through the testing of one variable (symbol word) at a time, as this is not a multivariable approach. The testing for each symbol word follows three price trend assumptions: (1) leading correlation to bullish price trends, (2) leading correlation to bearish price trends, and (3) leading correlation for both directions. As part of validating the hypothesis, the allowed time range for the start of a price trend is set to a three-week time range around the mean time distance, as this time range included 90 percent of the historical cases.

Cross-correlation is a useful technique for determining the time delay between two signals. After calculating, through an iterative fitting process, the cross-correlation between the two, the maximum of the cross-correlation function indicates the point in time where the signals are best aligned and confirms whether there is alignment with the graphically noted mean.[2]

Some restrictions were applied as part of the testing relating to the performance of the asset prices; there was no testing made nor did the hypothesis assume any scaled relationship between the magnitude of the spike and the magnitude of the price trend. Also, no conditions or testing were made on constants in terms of end time of a price trend, as this is not expected to share similarities among different asset classes nor between up and down trends as down trends typically play out a lot faster than up trends. There were, however, minimum conditions set on what constitutes an "approved" trend in terms of achieved return; long trade for a bull trend and short trade for a bear trend, over a specified time (specifically, after that minimum condition was met, the trend can continue in the same direction or it can reverse).

Testing the Time Series against Known Cycles

Although recurring cycles with regular frequencies are not known to exist in the psychological environment (nor did Jung ever indicate their existence for archetypes), they do activate spontaneously to rectify imbalances in the holistic mind. In testing we still attempt to pair the patterns of archetypal forces, manifested through symbol occurrences in media, with known cycles to investigate any possibility of match. Obviously with a limited time range of data to assess, traditional cycles such as the 45- to 60-year Kondratiev cycle, the 15- to 25-year Kuznets cycle, and the 7- to 11-year Juglar cycle cannot be tested. Thus the focus needs to be on shorter cycles, such as the 3- to 5-year Kitchin cycle or the shorter time range of the different Elliott waves.[3]

However, when applying those patterns and trying to match them with the spikes in the root symbol words, no significant levels of correlation exist. The outbursts of spikes in symbol words are simply too erratic in time and magnitude to match any obvious recurring or standardised patterns; the spikes occur in random patterns with little or no possibility, based on previous patterns, to project in time for the next spike.

This would, if accepting the hypothesis of the collective unconscious and archetypes as being drivers behind zeitgeists and what is considered to be irrational behaviour in the financial markets, explain why it is so difficult to forecast when the rational man theory should apply. It also makes the reliance on recurring patterns and/or cycles in technical analysis produce such lackluster performance. If the psychological fuel that feeds price trends and financial bubbles is dictated by the psychological perceptions provided by the *differing* archetypes that individually cannot be linked to any cyclical patterns, in the short term at least, the focus needs to be on a holistic approach in monitoring the individual archetypes equipped with the historical correlations between specific archetypes and financial assets.

Constructing Archetypal Composite Indexes

To achieve a comprehensive representation of all facets of an archetype, a composite index needs to be constructed. The composite index is developed around the root symbols that represent the key characteristics of each individual archetype, such as the archetype The Sun obviously being

FIGURE 8.4 Testing Auxiliary Symbol Words

The auxiliary symbol words act as validators to help distinguish between the true and false signals for the root symbol word

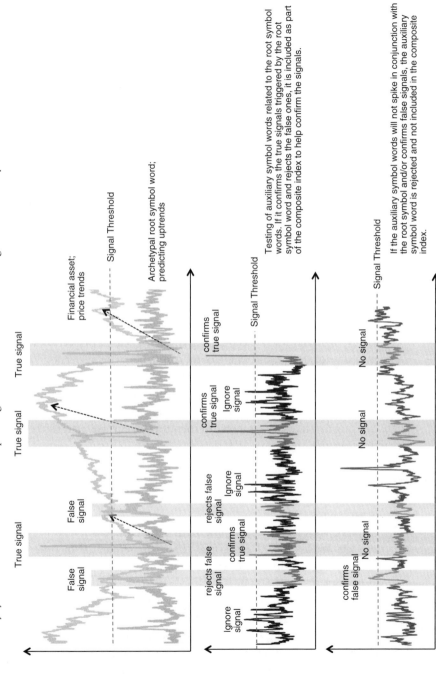

represented by the symbol word *sun* and its synonyms, The Warrior being represented by symbols representing a warrior or solider, and an archetypal activity like Birth being represented by birth-like symbols. Grammatically most archetypes are of a subject or object nature, with fewer being classified as verbs or adjectives. To these root symbols are then paired symbol words of an auxiliary nature that assist in describing the particular archetypes, not necessarily always with obvious links to the root symbols.

Creating a composite index also helps strengthen the archetypal hypothesis, if it can be demonstrated that these symbol words coincide over time in terms of noise and spike patterns. It will also help distinguish between true and false signals for the root symbols and thus comes to serve as a validating factor. To assess their efficiency, in addition to the qualitative review to conduct sense checks of the paired words, it has to be determined whether war- and peace-related archetype symbols spiking in parallel, and birth and death archetype symbols also spiking together, constitute a meaningful relationship or just a nonsense correlation. Randomly selected words are tested to determine if they help increase the success ratio in filtering out false signals and are then used as a benchmark comparison to help check for minimum levels of validity between true and false signals.

Initially, the root symbols are ranked by the success ratio in producing true versus false signals; these are typically asymmetric, either projecting upward or downward price trends, but rarely both. A notably wide dispersion among the root symbols and their synonyms provides evidence of inconsistencies. Given the asymmetrical characters of the archetypal force, antonym symbols can be used to *a certain degree* as reverse indicators, such as The Mother archetype representing a risk averse strategy, to then test for reverse patterns of symbols representing risk aggressive archetypes.

For each qualitatively approved root symbol, word correlation tests are then run, in the following order, against:

1. Its synonyms.
2. Auxiliary subjects, especially if a myth can be established and tested with time lags for associated archetypal characters sequential in time.
3. Auxiliary objects, including events; for the archetype The Warrior, they would include symbol words such as *sword*, *axe*, and *battlefield*.
4. Auxiliary verbs; for The Warrior examples include symbolic expressions such as "his proposal got *shot* down," "budget *cuts*," and "the home team *massacred* the visiting team and won the match."
5. Adjectives that describe the activated archetype; some are obviously related. For example, *strong* or *brave* connects naturally with The Warrior but most

adjectives have no natural relationship to the root symbol, so a comprehensive testing of all adjectives is required.

6. The root symbol's antonyms.
7. A sample of random words, which includes all symbol words with a significant correlation R-square value to produce a benchmark mapping.

This testing is conducted at each occasion a spike appears and is enhanced with an in-depth review of the articles containing the symbol words in question to ensure their validity. It is the root symbol's pattern that drives the index; whether its signals are considered true or false is confirmed by the components of the composite index. The composite index is therefore not presented as an econometric expression, in which the individual symbol words constitute the variables; rather it is to be viewed as a simplified neural network where the auxiliary symbol words confirming spikes distinguish the true ones from the false. Whereas the root symbol words' success ratio between true and false signals is critical to proceed with the archetype hypothesis, for the auxiliary symbol words no such restriction is applied, which means that certain of these in isolation can have success ratios that are quite low in projecting future price trends for the financial asset. It will still be part of the composite index as long as its spikes coincide with the root symbol word's true signals; therefore, this is the distinction between root symbols, with direct links to the archetype's core characteristics, and symbols in the periphery of the archetypes of importance in developing the model. Figure 8.4 provides a graphical depiction of the process.

Backtesting and Calibration

Backtesting and the subsequent calibration of the composite indexes are conducted as part of a regular biannual exercise but also in conjunction with spike signals, true as well as false, following the testing protocol as described in the previous section. The recurring backtesting will help ensure validity in the precursor status of the root symbol words and confirm that the leading, partial correlations hold true over time and also, at least in a circumstantial way, provide pointers towards a causal relationship between the trending of symbolic language and its orchestration of behaviour in the financial markets.

The performance of each composite index in successfully being able to predict a move in the financial asset is calculated and gauged against random outcomes to verify whether it produces an outcome that, by a significant number, beats chance and also identifies and investigates whether there are any symbol words that over time have shown a high level of leading correlation to a particular financial asset with no obvious relation. These "unrelated" symbol words with high correlation are dissected to establish no cases of contamination, so that only occurrences of the symbolic meaning are included and occurrences of the literal meaning are excluded. Synonyms are tested for correlation and if there are no such cases, the unrelated symbol words are written off as a random event.

Only symbols words that have triggered signals a multitude of times over the 2000–2013 test period are considered to have enough occurrences to ensure validity in the statistical tests, thus reducing the likelihood of correlation due to pure randomness given the scarcity of "testable" events.

The number of Type II errors versus the total number of signals is assessed to gauge and calibrate the signal threshold levels as well as the suitability of the root symbol word itself. For Type I errors, where a signal does not precede a confirmed price trend in the associated financial assets, if the level of Type I errors starts to exceed the 10 percent mark, a review of the validity of the root symbol and its synonyms is conducted to appraise its continued use as a representative symbol for the particular archetype. The assessment and low levels of acceptance of Types I and II errors, as well as requirements of parallel spikes for related symbols and assessing it versus chance over time, comprises the main elements of the testing framework.

Traditional testing metrics such as *Akaike Information criterion* and *Schwarz criterion* become less applicable as the number of auxiliary symbol words acting as validators of signals do not form part of an econometric model, so more of them do not cause information entropy; it is the opposite. The more popularised the symbolic use of certain themes has become, and subsequently the stronger influence on thought patterns and behaviour, more rather than less symbol words should spike in frequency of usage and reduce the likelihood of random events. Therefore, a metric that relates the number of symbol words spiking versus its total word universe provides assistance in understanding strength of influence. The key part of that testing includes running correlation tests to corroborate a single symbol word's spike with its synonyms or symbols that cluster within the same archetypal theme; any lack of high correlations would reject the signal as false.

Conclusion

With a cleansed population of symbol words designed and collated as expressed in Chapters 6 and 7, statistical testing can commence with a view to establish whether a recurring leading correlation exists between clusters of archetypal symbol words and particular financial assets. A structured testing protocol and associated calibration and routine backtesting enhance identification of the most appropriate levels of correlation.

Notes

1. J. R. Pierce, *An Introduction to Information Theory: Symbols, Signals and Noise* (Dover Books on Mathematics) (Mineola, NY: Dover Publications, 1980).
2. John Y. Campbell, Andrew W. Lo, and A. Craig MacKinlay, *The Econometrics of Financial Markets* (Princeton, NJ: Princeton University Press, 1996).
3. E. R. Dewey and E. F. Dakin, *Cycles: The Science of Prediction* (Eastford, CT: Martino Fine Books, 2010).

References

Dewey, E. R., and E. F. Dakin. 2010. *Cycles: The Science of Prediction*. Eastford, CT: Martino Fine Books.

Campbell, John Y., Andrew W. Lo, and A. Craig MacKinlay. 1996. *The Econometrics of Financial Markets*. Princeton, NJ: Princeton University Press.

Pierce, J. R. 1980. *An Introduction to Information Theory: Symbols, Signals and Noise* (Dover Books on Mathematics) Mineola, NY: Dover Publications.

CHAPTER 9

Examples of Archetypal Influences on the Formation of Financial Bubbles

When reviewing recent examples of financial bubbles—such as the dot-com bubble crash in 2001 and the US property bubble collapse in 2007—applying Jungian archetypes to how the events unfolded, one can point to the influences of particular archetypes providing the psychological fuel that helped develop and sustain these bubbles. To be clear about the role of archetypes, the actual development of Internet-related technologies and companies and the changing business model that the New Economy triggered are in themselves not a product of archetypes. These technological innovations are unrelated to the reigning psychological environment.

Archetypes impact the direction of the changed perceptions that emerge with the introduction of a new technology. Through prompting a new zeitgeist, archetypes equip the collective human mind with a better perception to handle the changing realities and the accompanying paradigm shift. However it carries the risk to, in the short term, as part of the archetypal energy entering the conscious, lead to excessive psychological manifestations such as the hysteria and panics commonly seen as part of a bubble formation. These investment behaviours reside once the archetype has become fully integrated into the collective mind and a new holistic mental balance has been established.

The dot-com bubble and the US property bubble will here serve as case studies, which are part of a comprehensive ongoing systematic review of all major bubbles from the twentieth century onwards. However, ensuring access to media outlets extensive enough to perform a statistical symbol analysis remains a challenge to be addressed and thus this publication can only focus on these two cases studies.

The key psychological theme that triggered the dot-com bubble and that was underpinned by archetypes was the belief that anything Internet related had assumed alchemical characteristics, in the end so extreme that just adding the prefix *e-* (for "electronic") to a corporate name (so-called prefix investing) could make that company's share price shoot straight up. Anything Internet related became the making of gold. In the case of the property bubble, the changing psychological factor was the view that property prices always go up, despite a lack of historical support for such an assumption, creating a hysteria that held very few skeptics.

Research into the causes of bubbles is not conclusive; it is true that easy access to money tends to trigger asset bubbles. However, bubbles occurred even with no loose monetary policy and vice versa. Some research suggests that it is the price momentum itself that triggers liquidity.[1]

It is also true that the introduction of new technology drives speculation and an optimistic view in terms of upward price trends for related companies. However, from the valuation perspective, it is really only the 1929 crash, in part driven by the excessive optimism around the new technology of the day, and the 2001 dot-com crash, that took it to such levels that it impacted the entire stock market's mood. This kind of all-encompassing bubble hysteria and subsequent valuations and parabolic price patterns were not noted for other technology-related introductions, such as the biotech revolution of the early 1980s, or the electronics boom of the early 1960s, or the 1890s railway boom, where the speculative mood was generally constrained to the specific industry and did not spread to the overall market, as can be noted in Figure 9.1.[2]

An interesting psychological phenomenon is the zeitgeist-constrained rationality that leads to the denial of the existence of a bubble, even, if by historical benchmarks, it should have been acknowledged. This reduction of perceptive abilities during the height of the bubble was perhaps best high-lighted by Queen Elizabeth's questions to economists in the aftermath of the property bubble: "Why did nobody notice it?"[3] And even for individuals fully recognising the existence of a bubble, they still could not withdraw from the force of the archetype and kept feeding the bubble; fund managers, despite the career risk, ran with the herd and did not deviate in benchmark performance, despite personal doubts on the continuation of the price trends.

FIGURE 9.1   Crash of 1929 and 2001

Looking at the US stock market from a valuation perspective as highlighted in the chart; two bubbles stand out in particular with their characteristic parabolic price formations: the 1929 crash and the dot-com crash of 2001.

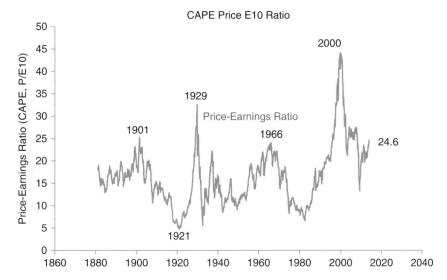

Source: Robert Shiller data sources, stock market data www.econ.yale.edu/~shiller/data.htm.

To support the constrained rationality, a number of defense mechanisms come into play and rationalisation is used to uphold the bubble behaviour aligned with the zeitgeist. Once the bubble has burst, projections and scapegoats are identified and one's own feelings of guilt are transferred onto others—whether it is projecting it on individual persons, groups, or the market economy as a whole—and eventually a holistic mental balance can be restored.

Whereas the archetype is concerned only with the bubble formation as a manifestation of its energy levels, a bubble's effect on the real economy after the crash depends on other factors such as levels of credit, extent of contagion to other markets, existing regulatory framework, and so on. Hence the aftermath of the dot-com bubble was relatively mild on the economy as a whole compared to that of the 1929 crash and the 2007 US property bubble crash. The predictive capabilities of studying the archetypal symbols lies in identifying recurring precursors in terms of when the uptrend leg of the bubble starts and possibly also providing clues on when the price bubble is about to pop.

From the case studies included in this chapter and lacking the systematic approach, it is not possible to determine whether the specific archetypes causing these bubbles are part of a greater narrative that is being played out and the formation of decades-long archetypes that potentially could explain triggers behind neoliberal monetary policy and the maternal perspective of the welfare state replacing the night-watchman state, which contained paternal characteristics.

The Dot-Com Bubble

The dot-com bubble started to form in about 1995, taking the characteristics of a mania in mid-1998 and having a definite peak on March 10, 2000, when the technology-focused NASDAQ index hit an all-time high, after a more than four-fold increase since 1996 with the individual Internet index increasing almost 1,000 percent. Over the following two years, it ended up retracting all its gain almost to the starting point of the price rise; in all, it followed a typical financial bubble formation (see Figure 9.2). Individual stocks within the TMT sector (technology, media, and telecom) saw even more remarkable developments in terms of stock price upward movement, and on the way down many of them ended up in bankruptcy.

Warnings about the unrealistic valuations were ignored. Federal Reserve Chairman Alan Greenspan referred to the term *irrational exuberance* in a comment to the stock market in 1996. Warren Buffett warned repeatedly that the TMT sector was in a bubble formation that eventually would end in a crash. Obviously neither of them could provide any timing of the price bubble implosion.

At the peak of the dot-com hysteria, just adding the prefix *e-* or a *.com* ending to a company's name could trigger an immediate increase in share price. It was not unusual for individual Internet stocks to increase by 20 to 30 percent on a single day; on the down turn of the bubble, the price drops could be of greater magnitude than that. These fast moves in the up-phase of the bubble led to many quick fortunes being built and triggered plenty of people leaving their careers or studies to take up stock trading for the first time or pursue full-time day-trading in and out of mainly Internet-related stocks, preferably with margin. These activities helped to push up trading volumes to unprecedented highs.

The craze of the mania made it possible to list dot-com companies that never made any profits and in some examples hardly even had revenues.

FIGURE 9.2 NASDAQ Price Trend Highlighting the Formation of a Bubble between 1998 and 2002

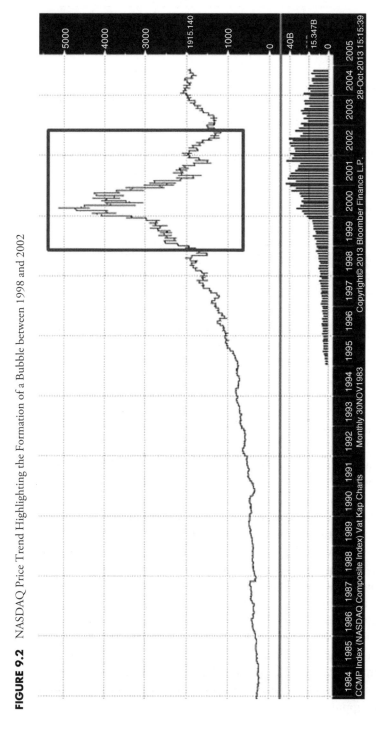

Source: Bloomberg L. P.

The fact that most of these companies had never been profitable forced changes to valuation methodologies; the focus had to be on various growth metrics as there were no profits. This meant that a term such as *burn rate*, the amount of money a company was spending on expanding its network, became an important metric. The more it spent, the more valuable it became; hence, achieving high burn rates and similar measurements led to Internet start-ups heavily indebting themselves in an attempt to achieve higher hit rates and numbers of visitors to their websites. This perverted effect obviously led to an even earlier demise for these companies because their revenues never could match the increasing debts, due to the dot-com business models relying on quickly building up a market share online and, through economies of scale, becoming the dominant player in a given niche, whether selling pet food or fashion, thus forcing other online and traditional retailers out of business. The evolution of Amazon and Google largely followed this model, and as the dominant players in their specific areas, they achieved premium earnings. To lure in customers, these companies offered services for free, but once their dominant positions had been established and competition had been forced out, they started to charge for their services or command premium fees for advertising space. In such a context, achieving a high burn rate to speed up the gaining of market share became a sensible strategy. Lacking earnings, concepts such as *mind share*, the level of consumer awareness of any brand, became a valuation metric seen as a gauge for future earnings.

The interpretation of the quick price appreciations for dot-com stocks differed; proponents of the *Efficient Market Hypothesis* were generally at a loss to explain how the stock market could assign multibillion-dollar market caps to companies that never made any profits. Others took a lottery-ticket approach to valuing dot-com stocks. These were seen as high-risk ventures in which most would go bankrupt but if one bought enough, the few winners would make up for the many losses, and therefore at a portfolio-approach level, this could prove to be a profitable strategy. However, unlike lottery tickets there were no absolute due dates and the listed dot-com companies could be traded on a daily basis and with moves in double digit percentages not uncommon, it became a difficult strategy to execute.

In the behavioural finance camp, the view was that this ultimately proved the efficient market hypothesis erroneous and pointed to herding behaviour as the key driver in the formation of the dot-com price bubble. However, the behavioural finance theorists were not able to explain why this hype was different than other paradigm shifts; in fact many of them seemed to be drawn into the very zeitgeist that was behind the bubble, referring to the unique investment approach of the New Economy.

A few academics took, in hindsight, a psychoanalytical view and regarded the dot-com stocks as "fantastic objects," meaning idealised infantile objects due to Oedipal rivalry. However, the review was left there, without further empirical research or studies.

In the aftermath of the bubble, the typical hunt for scapegoats started, and generally much blame fell on the investment banks that were accused of using IPOs (initial public offerings) to take to market immature companies, that is, those in terms of revenue or prospects, incapable of ever making any earnings and whose prospectus lacked proper due diligence. Indeed there were also some fraudulent cases, where financial statements had been manipulated and in some cases through the participation or at least acknowledgement by the sponsoring investment banks. However, it was the enormous demand for listed dot-com stocks from the general public, either through direct investments or institutional arrangements, that the investment banks responded to. And the poor economics of these dot-com firms and in most cases hopeless future outlooks in terms of survival were generally all in the IPO prospectus, although often glossed over with flashy presentations. However, any traditional valuation methods would have rated these companies at best as highly speculative "lottery tickets" with little chance of winning in the long run, a notion that was not lost on investors such as Warren Buffett. For the investors, it was the dot-com companies' alchemical characteristics that were the great allure, and little attention was paid to the IPO prospectus or financial statements.

So, whereas the evolution of the Internet and the commercialisation of it were well grounded in actual technical developments, an archetypal influence from the collective unconscious allowed a hype to form that eventually lead to a market-wide excessive price bubble.[4]

The Archetypal Driver to the Dot-Com Bubble

The psychological driver behind the dot-com bubble was the perception and fantasy that investing in anything Internet related was alchemical; it took on the magical dimension of making gold out of base metals. This belief became embedded in the herding instincts that kept prices going up until they reached parabolic proportions. The archetype that triggers such thinking is that of The Wizard or similar synonyms such as The Alchemist or The Magician. By reviewing symbolic occurrences, testing through the various archetypes, establishing which ones preceded the price bubble, and monitoring how these performed during and after the bubble, we gain indications of an archetype that has activated and is about to influence thought patterns and behaviour aligned with the characteristics of the particular archetype. If a precursive correlation between themes of symbol words and the price trend of an asset can be identified, following the testing protocol as outlined in Chapter 8, a sense check is conducted to assess the validity of the characteristics of the archetype and correlated asset in question. Ideally, if a recurring pattern of correlation over time can be demonstrated, it provides further support to the hypothesis as does the clustering of synonyms spiking in parallel to reduce the risk of random correlations.

When performing correlation tests between the various symbol words and the NASDAQ index representing the dot-com bubble, The Wizard symbol and its synonyms appear, as depicted in Figure 9.3, highlight leading correlation and distinctive spikes, providing commercial opportunities to time the mania part of the bubble.

The Wizard archetype, and its synonyms, The Alchemist, The Sage, The Magician, The Wise Man, and The Druid, and related symbolic subjects, verbs, and adjectives demonstrate spikes closely aligned in time with a lack of deviations and outliers. This provides circumstantial evidence of a sudden drastic use of such symbolic language, indicating the activation of the

FIGURE 9.3 The Wizard and Its Synonyms' Symbol Theme as a Precursor to the Bubble Formation of Dot-Com Stocks

archetype. Other related archetypes but distinctively different in nature, such as The Trickster, The Clown, The Joker, The Jester, and The Fool did not spike in tandem with The Wizard cluster nor did their animal representations such as The Monkey and The Fox. So through testing the symbol activity for each particular archetype, one can pin down quite precisely the archetype activating and the ones that remain dormant.

So what are the characteristics of The Wizard and what are the psychological mechanisms that trigger it?

The Wizard archetype activates to help the mind adapt to a new reality and provide a change in perception to deal with a paradigm shift in the real world, such as the technology and business changes that the Internet brought with it, and that the existing mind-set is not equipped to handle. The characteristics of The Wizard include alchemical aspirations, the metaphorical transformation of base metal into gold through magical features. This symbolic transformation is manifested in reality through the paradigm shift in question, which leads to unrealistic fantasies on the output of such, the dot-com companies, and the making of gold through this transformation. The dot-coms become a magical part that serves this gold-making fantasy and the demand for this fantasy increases until it reaches manic levels. This tends to lead to hysteria, and Jung refers to this kind of archetype as a *mania* personality. Once the integration of the archetype into the conscious part of the mind is completed, the hysteria resides and the archetype becomes dormant again as the collective mind has incorporated the paradigm shift into its conscious make-up which then becomes a transformation of the mind itself. Therefore, the outmoded thinking through this archetypal force is torn down and a new mindset is built.[5]

Looking at other societal trends at that time to detect The Wizard characterisation obviously serves only as anecdotal evidence, because it is difficult to statistically quantify, and the time lag between societal trends and stock market trends and the activation of an archetype differs quite significantly. With the former adapting at a slower pace, such as fashion generally being seasonal, cultural expressions through literature and film take a longer time to manifest and be absorbed by the general public than the establishment of a trend in the financial markets, through their real-time pricing in which a new long-term trend can shift over a matter of months; in contrast, in the cultural world, the response time is likely years. So cultural manifestations of the early twenty-first century did see a popularisation of The Wizard archetype characteristics, as displayed through the enormous popularity of the Lord of the Rings movie franchise as well as the best-selling Harry Potter books and movies.

To definitely establish The Wizard as an archetype preceding bubbles or strong price trends in paradigm shifts, one would have to study media sources stretching back from the 1850s onwards, with symbol word spikes preceding the mania of the 1929 bubble and possibly prior to the 1890s railway rally and the early 1960s electronics boom. Also, being able to determine magic as a popular form of entertainment around those time epoch could provide additional support to the theory. An appearance of The Wizard archetype symbol word spike with no correlation to the uptrends of technology stocks over that time period would help disregard the hypothesis. The alchemical part of this particular archetype obviously bears obvious links with gold itself; however, additional symbol attributes, such as The Sun marking an alignment with gold needs to spike in tandem with The Wizard/Alchemist archetype. These were, however, not present in this case.

The end of the dot-com bubble was preceded by a number of death-related symbol words, in this particular case clustered around the symbolic use of words such as *choking, suffocating, strangle,* and similar words; however, no words such as *drowning* or *amputation* spiked in parallel. If this was part of the greater narrative, indicating the arrival of The Wizard archetypal thought patterns into the conscious part of the mind, completing the establishment of a

FIGURE 9.4 The Symbolic Use of the Word *Choking* and Similar Words Preceding the Drastic Collapse of the Dot-Com Bubble

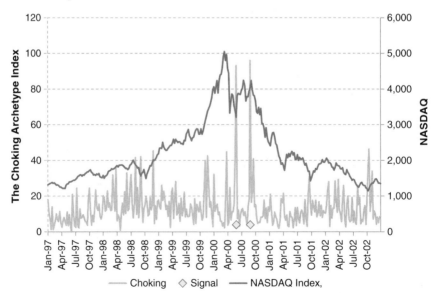

new holistic equilibrium of the mind, the hysteria residing and approaching the valuation of dot-com companies in accordance with traditional valuation metrics, is only speculative. However, an archetype returning to a dormant level is often marked through an excess in use of birth, rebirth, or death symbolic terminology, or in other cases, as for the US property bubble, the archetype shifts in character (see Figure 9.4).

The US Property Bubble

The housing bubbles in the United States took off from a temporary bottom in prices in 1997, initiating the bubble trend from a then all-time high in property prices in 2000, and with a peak in prices in 2006 with the down leg of the bubble still hitting new low levels in 2012 (see Figure 9.5). The housing prices between 2000 and 2006 went up almost 70 percent, deviating considerably from the historically 0.4 percent per annum. The credit crisis that followed the downfall in property prices is generally regarded as the leading cause of the severe recession that followed in the United States.

A number of causes of the property bubble were pointed out; among them were the low interest rates and lax regulatory and lending standards allowing mortgages to be given to groups with traditionally low credit scores and people highly likely to become delinquent on servicing their mortgages. Most important was the change in the assumption that property prices would always go up, or at least never go down, a sentiment publicly shared by leading industry practitioners, politicians, academics, and regulators such as the US Federal Reserve Chairman Ben Bernanke, as highlighted in the following interview transcription:

7/1/05—Interview on CNBC

Interviewer: Tell me, what is the worst-case scenario? We have so many economists coming on our air saying, "Oh, this is a bubble, and it's going to burst, and this is going to be a real issue for the economy." Some say it could even cause a recession at some point. What is the worst-case scenario if in fact we were to see prices come down substantially across the country?

Bernanke: Well, I guess I don't buy your premise. It's a pretty unlikely possibility. We've never had a decline in house prices on a nationwide basis. So, what I think what is more likely is that house prices will slow, maybe stabilize, might slow consumption spending a bit. I don't think it's gonna drive the economy too far from its full employment path, though.[6]

FIGURE 9.5 A Highlight of US Property Prices from 1890 to 2004

Property prices are compared to population, building costs, and bond yields. The inflation-adjusted US home prices increased by 0.4 percent annually during the measurement period. The home prices show low correlation with US stock price trends.

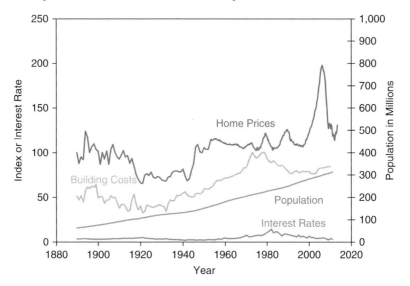

Source: Robert Shiller data sources, historical housing market data www.econ.yale.edu/ ~shiller/data.htm.

This almost consensus assumption triggered a speculative momentum and an urge to aspire to home ownership rather than renting. Purchasing condominiums while still being constructed and then selling them without ever living in them, became commonplace, a speculative pattern differing from previous eras. These speculations were underpinned by easy access to mortgages. The housing bubble affected mostly residential properties and about half of the US states were impacted. Eventually, starting in 2006, homeowners, through overextending their borrowing capacity and being unable to make their mortgage payments, triggered an increase in foreclosures, leading to prices weakening and then starting to drop with the S&P Shiller-Case housing index that saw its largest year-to-year drop in 2008.

The high levels of debt helped hasten the downtrend when refinancing became increasingly difficult; households had become increasingly indebted, with property as the main collateral. The debt ratio to disposable personal income rose from 77 percent in 1990 to 127 percent at the end of 2007, with much of the increase related to mortgages. Finance companies securitised these mortgages into structured financial products carrying acronyms such as MBS (mortgage backed securities) and CDS (credit default swaps), selling out tranches that in hindsight carried a lot higher default risk than the risk models and ratings had factored in, based on the assumption of forever-increasing property prices and low correlations of defaults between different markets. That is, prices would not fall and they definitely would not fall at the same time. At the height of the bubble, skeptical voices, such as those of Warren Buffett and the US academic Robert Shiller, were ignored. They warned about the assumption that house prices could not fall and clearly pointed out the contagious optimism that kept fueling the bubble.[7]

As Warren Buffett noted: "There was the greatest bubble I've ever seen in my life. . . . The entire American public eventually was caught up in a belief that housing prices could not fall dramatically."[8]

The typical hunt for scapegoats occurred after the collapse of the bubble, blaming mortgage lenders for lax lending policies and, in the subsequent credit crisis that followed, blaming banks and rating agencies responsible for selling financial products related to the securitised mortgages that did not correctly reflect the actual high risk they carried. In the end, blame was assigned to the whole capitalistic system, the market economy.

However, the psychological driver to the property bubble was a change in perception of increasing property prices, which altered the view on properties that took a speculative pattern, rarely seen historically in the United States. This speculation eventually evolved into hysteria and the strong demand made access to capital easy, making returns on the less and less needed equity invested per property more attractive. So what was the archetypal force that changed the perception to the belief of increasing property prices and that triggered the mania that drove property prices up to bubble levels?

The Archetypal Driver to the US Property Bubble

Properties as an asset class are, from the archetypal perspective, regarded as a female-maternal manifestation, especially when considering home ownership rather than construction. The testing of female-maternal-related archetypal symbol words versus property prices should demonstrate correlation; however, the female archetypes come in different forms (see Figure 9.6).

The female-maternal archetypal character that highlights the regal aspects is the Empress or its synonyms, the Queen and the Matriarch, and associated symbols represented as subjects, objects, verbs, and adjectives, highlighting female royal symbolic language. The archetype generally represents the peak of the maternal archetype before it shifts to a shadow character and eventually is replaced by something else that manifests through the withdrawal of female

FIGURE 9.6   The Empress Archetype

The Empress archetype and synonyms-related symbol words as a precursor to the US property bubble are represented through the Dow Jones Real Estate Index (DJUSRE). The Empress archetype is likely the extension and crowning height of the decades-long activated maternal archetype.

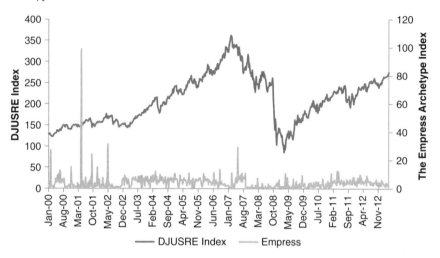

thought structures in the psychological environment. It is the source of welfare thinking and materialism. The Empress archetype exacerbates all aspects female and maternal as the reigning perception of reality, crowding out other thought patterns and leading to excesses in maternal-related asset classes, in particular the drive towards home ownership and the positive outlook to that asset class, drastically increasing the probability of price bubbles. Contemporary societal trends promote feminine thinking, such as gender and women's studies in academics, affirmative action advancing women in leadership roles, and *Sex and the City*–like entertainment and lifestyle. All are the manifestation of the activation of the Empress archetype.

Eventually replacing the Empress archetype, as it leads to unbalances in the collective holistic mind, is at first a female shadow character that diminishes the power of the female archetype thought pattern and eventually is replaced with another, not necessarily a contrasting male-paternal archetype, but a complementary one to seek an equilibrium in the psychological context.

The activation of such a shadow aspect of the female-maternal archetype should mark a shift in the positive sentiment that promoted property investment and kept pushing the price bubble upwards and indicates the downturn of the bubble.

FIGURE 9.7   The Harlot Archetype

Replacing the Empress reflection of the maternal archetype is the Harlot theme symbolism, which occurred at the end of 2007. It represents a shadow side of feminism and spells the likely end of the maternal archetypal thought patterns and behaviour.

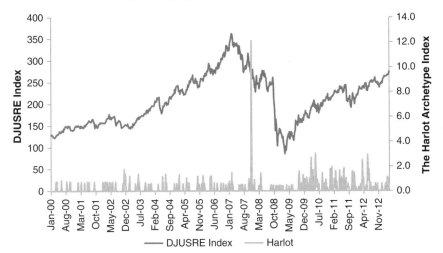

The transition is from the height of the female-maternal archetype in the form of the Empress, to less positive characteristics of maternal symbolism, such as the Harlot archetype and its synonyms, The Terrible Mother, the Witch, and the Femme Fatale, and associated symbolic language (see Figure 9.7). This archetype not only marks the end of the female-mother archetype reign but also the end of the positive views of any investment classes associated with it. The Harlot archetypes also mark a shift from thinking about welfare and materialism towards sentiments of fear, danger, darkness, dismemberment, emasculation, death, destruction, and lack of emotional evolvement.[9]

Conclusion

The review of the dot-com and US property bubbles and their link to a cluster of archetypal symbol words preceding major price trends helps to better understand the influence from unconscious sentiments that might not appear obvious in a traditional cause-effect review. Existing correlation, as well as anecdotal evidence, lead to insights that help further progress the research, albeit with many questions remaining to be answered.

Notes

1. Albert Edwards, "Lies, Rhubarb, Poppycock, Bilge, Utter Nonsense, Caravans and Liquidity," Dresdner Kleinworth Global Strategy Report, January 16, 2007, www .fullermoney.com/content/2007–01–22/AlbertEdwardsOnLiquidityGlobal_ Strat-147655-N.pdf (accessed November 30, 2013); Carmen M. Reinhart and Kenneth Rogoff, *This Time Is Different: Eight Centuries of Financial Folly*, reprint ed. (Princeton, NJ: Princeton University Press, 2011) (accessed November 30, 2013); Carmen M. Reinhart and Kenneth Rogoff, "From Financial Crash to Debt Crisis" (NBER Working Paper No. 15795, 2010), www.nber.org/papers/w15795 (accessed November 30, 2013); Jeffrey A. Franke and George Saravelos, "Are Leading Indicators of Financial Crises Useful for Assessing Country Vulnerability? Evidence from the 2008–09 Global Crisis" (NBER Working Paper No. 16047, 2010), www.nber.org/papers/w16047 (accessed November 30, 2013).
2. Bubble.com, "All Technological Revolutions Carry Risks as Well as Rewards," *The Economist*, September 21, 2000, www.economist.com/node/375561 (accessed November 30, 2013); Burton G. Malkiel, *A Random Walk Down Wall Street: The Time-Tested Strategy for Successful Investing*, 10th ed. (New York: W. W. Norton & Company, 2012).
3. Andrew Pierce, "The Queen Asks Why No One Saw the Credit Crunch Coming," *The Telegraph* November 5, 2008, www.telegraph.co.uk/news/uknews /theroyalfamily/3386353/The-Queen-asks-why-no-one-saw-the-credit-crunch-coming.html (accessed November 30, 2013).
4. Elizabeth K. Keating, Thomas Z. Lys, and Robert P. Magee, "The Internet Downturn: Finding Valuation Factors in Spring 2000," JAE Boston Conference, June 2001, http://papers.ssrn.com/sol3/papers.cfm?abstract_id=262441 (accessed November 30, 2013); Jonathan Lewellen, "Discussion of 'The Internet Downturn: Finding Valuation Factors in Spring 2000,'" *Journal of Accounting and Economics* 34 (2003): 237–247; Richard J. Taffler and David A. Tuckett, "A Psychoanalytic Interpretation of Dot.Com Stock Valuations," version 5.4, March 1, 2005, http:// papers.ssrn.com/sol3/papers.cfm?abstract_id=676635 (accessed November 30, 2013); Richard J. Taffler and David A. Tuckett, "Internet Stocks as 'Phantastic Objects': A Psychoanalytic Interpretation of Shareholder Valuation during Dot. Com Mania," version 2, July 3, 2002, https://dspace.lib.cranfield.ac.uk/bitstream/ 1826/3272/1/Internet%20Stocks%20as%20phantastic%20objects-2003.pdf (accessed November 30, 2013); Charles P. Kindleberger and Robert Z. Aliber, *Manias, Panics and Crashes: A History of Financial Crises*, 6th ed. (New York: Palgrave Macmillan, 2011); Roger Lowenstein, *Origins of the Crash: The Great Bubble and Its Undoing* (New York: Penguin Books, 2004); Florian Galler, "Group Process and Stock Markets: 2002 to 2009," *Journal of Psychohistory* 37, no. 2 (2009) http://www .psychohistory.ch/Group%20Process%20And%20Stock%20Markets%202002% 20-%202009.pdf (accessed November 30, 2013).

5. Jolande Jacobi, *Complex/Archetype/Symbol in the Psychology of C. G. Jung* (Bollingen Series, 57) (Princeton, NJ: Princeton University Press, 1971); C. G. Jung, *The Archetypes and the Collective Unconscious* (Vol. 9, Part 1 of *The Collected Works of C. G. Jung*), ed. R. F. C. Hull, 2nd ed. (Princeton, NJ: Princeton University Press, 1981); C. G. Jung, *Four Archetypes*, ed. R. F. C. Hull, Bollingen Series XX, Vol. 9, Part 1 of *The Collected Works of C. G. Jung* (Princeton, NJ: Princeton University Press, 2010); John Granrose, "The Archetype of the Magician" (diploma thesis, C. G. Jung Institute, Zürich, 1996), www.granrose.com/main/articles/thesis.html (accessed November 30, 2013).

6. Centre for Economic and Policy Research, Ben Bernanke interview on CNBC, July 1, 2005, www.cepr.net/index.php/bernanke-greatest-hits (accessed November 30, 2013).

7. Robert J. Shiller, *Irrational Exuberance*, 2nd ed. (New York: Crown Business, 2006); Steven Gjerstad and Vernon L. Smith, "From Bubble to Depression," *Wall Street Journal*, April 6, 2009; Vernon L. Smith, "Mired in Disequilibrium," *Newsweek*, January 24, 2011; Stan J. Liebowitz, "Anatomy of a Train Wreck: Causes of the Mortgage Meltdown," Independent Policy Report, Independent Institute, October 3, 2008, www.independent.org/pdf/policy_reports/2008–10–03-trainwreck.pdf (accessed November 30, 2013).

8. C-span.org, Financial Crisis Inquiry Commission, Warren Buffett Testimony, June 2, 2010.

9. Jung, *Four Archetypes*; Jacobi, *Complex/Archetype/Symbol in the Psychology of C. G. Jung*; Jung, *The Archetypes and the Collective Unconscious*.

References

Bubble.com. 2000. "All Technological Revolutions Carry Risks as Well as Rewards." *The Economist*, September 21. www.economist.com/node/375561 (accessed November 30, 2013).

Cassidy, John. 2003. *Dot.con: How America Lost Its Mind and Money in the Internet Era*. New York: Harper Perennial.

Centre for Economic and Policy Research. Ben Bernanke interview on CNBC, July 1, 2005. www.cepr.net/index.php/bernanke-greatest-hits (accessed November 30, 2013).

C-span.org. 2010. Financial Crisis Inquiry Commission, Warren Buffett Testimony, June 2.

Edwards, Albert. 2007. "Lies, Rhubarb, Poppycock, Bilge, Utter Nonsense, Caravans and Liquidity." Dresdner Kleinworth Global Strategy Report, January 16. www.fullermoney.com/content/2007–01–22/AlbertEdwardsOnLiquidityGlobal_Strat-147655-N.pdf (accessed November 30, 2013).

Franke, Jeffrey A., and George Saravelos. 2010. "Are Leading Indicators of Financial Crises Useful for Assessing Country Vulnerability? Evidence from the 2008–09 Global Crisis." NBER Working Paper No. 16047. www.nber.org/papers/w16047 (accessed November 30, 2013).

Galler, Florian. "Group Process and Stock Markets: 2002 to 2009." *Journal of Psychohistory* 37 no. 2. www.psychohistory.ch/Group%20Process%20And%20Stock%20Markets%202002%20-%202009.pdf (accessed November 30, 2013).

Gjerstad, Steven, and Vernon L. Smith. 2009. "From Bubble to Depression." *Wall Street Journal*, April 6.

Granrose, John. 1996. "The Archetype of the Magician." Diploma thesis. C. G. Jung Institute. Zürich. www.granrose.com/main/articles/thesis.html (accessed November 30, 2013).

Jacobi, Jolande. 1971. *Complex/Archetype/Symbol in the Psychology of C. G. Jung*. Bollingen Series, 57. Princeton, NJ: Princeton University Press.

Jung, C. G. 1981. *The Archetypes and the Collective Unconscious*. Vol. 9, Part 1 of *The Collected Works of C. G. Jung*. Translated by R. F. C. Hull. 2nd ed. Princeton, NJ: Princeton University Press.

———. 2010. *Four Archetypes*. Bollingen Series XX: Vol. 9, Part 1 of *The Collected Works of C. G. Jung*. Princeton, NJ: Princeton University Press.

Keating, Elizabeth K., Thomas Z. Lys, and Robert P. Magee. 2001. "The Internet Downturn: Finding Valuation Factors in Spring 2000." *JAE Boston Conference*, June. http://papers.ssrn.com/sol3/papers.cfm?abstract_id=262441 (accessed November 30, 2013).

Kindleberger, Charles P., and Robert Z. Aliber. 2011. *Manias, Panics and Crashes: A History of Financial Crises*. 6th ed. New York: Palgrave Macmillan.

Lewellen, Jonathan. 2003. Discussion of "The Internet Downturn: Finding Valuation Factors in Spring 2000." *Journal of Accounting and Economics* 34.

Liebowitz, Stan J. 2008. "Anatomy of a Train Wreck: Causes of the Mortgage Meltdown." Independent Policy Report. The Independent Institute, October 3. www.independent.org/pdf/policy_reports/2008–10–03-trainwreck.pdf (accessed November 30, 2013).

Malkiel, Burton G. 2012. *A Random Walk Down Wall Street: The Time-Tested Strategy for Successful Investing*. 10th ed. New York: W. W. Norton & Company.

Pierce, Andrew. 2008. "The Queen Asks Why No One Saw the Credit Crunch Coming." *The Telegraph*, November 5. www.telegraph.co.uk/news/uknews/theroyalfamily/3386353/The-Queen-asks-why-no-one-saw-the-credit-crunch-coming.html (accessed November 30, 2013).

Reinhart, Carmen M., and Kenneth Rogoff. 2010. "From Financial Crash to Debt Crisis." NBER Working Paper No. 15795. www.nber.org/papers/w15795 (accessed November 30, 2013).

———. 2011. *This Time Is Different: Eight Centuries of Financial Folly*. Reprint ed. Princeton, NJ: Princeton University Press.

Shiller, Robert J. 2006. *Irrational Exuberance*. 2nd ed. New York: Crown Business.

Robert Shiller data sources. Historical housing market data. http://www.econ.yale.edu/~shiller/data.htm (accessed November 30, 2013).

———. Stock market data. http://www.econ.yale.edu/~shiller/data.htm (accessed November 30, 2013).

Smith, Vernon L."Mired in Disequilibrium." *Newsweek*, January 24.

Taffler, Richard J., and David A. Tuckett. 2002. "Internet Stocks as 'Phantastic Objects': A Psychoanalytic Interpretation of Shareholder Valuation during Dot.Com Mania," version 2. July 3. https://dspace.lib.cranfield.ac.uk/bitstream/1826/3272/1/Internet%20Stocks%20as%20phantastic%20objects-2003.pdf (accessed November 30, 2013).

———. 2005. "A Psychoanalytic Interpretation of Dot.Com Stock Valuations," version 5.4. March 1. http://papers.ssrn.com/sol3/papers.cfm?abstract_id=676635.

CHAPTER 10

Conclusion

Wer den Zeitgeist heiratet, wird schnell Witwe (Who marries the Zeitgeist will soon be a widow.)

—German proverb

It is almost 100 years since Jung introduced the concepts of the collective unconscious and archetypes, which were mainly practically applied as part of his analytical psychology to deal with individual patients, helping them address neurotic behaviour by achieving a holistic balance in the mind. He did, however, occasionally comment on the archetypes' impact on society at large and how they could form the psychological foundation that dictates the zeitgeist of the time epoch. Jung's writings stopped at providing anecdotal evidence and case studies to his observations; there was never any comprehensive empirical testing that could be objectively verifiable to back his claims. Nevertheless, the concepts of archetypes and the collective unconscious were broadly accepted as an explanatory model of the mind by the psychology community, and it is only in the past decade that neuroscientific research has started to back the concepts of innate thought patterns, similar to what Jung proposed, although still not in a conclusive form.

The progress in neuroscience makes the proposition of archetypes attractive from the point of further empirical research; however, with the question of causation still looming, it is now worthwhile to look at correlations between assumed thought patterns and their influence on behaviour.

While there were ambiguities in the archetypal definition and scope throughout Jung's career, he did point to a finite number of archetypes that he identified among dreams, the study of myths, and folklore, and by drawing out common denominators. As the archetypes residing in the unconscious cannot be directly observed, Jung proposed that studying their tangible footprints—symbols that represent the various facets of an archetype, seemingly appearing spontaneously, as graphical representations in art work such as contents of dreams or figurative language such as metaphors and proverbs—would give an indication of the archetype at work.

How Archetypes Play Out

An archetype is either dormant or active and once it becomes active, its symbolic expressions start to increase and through monitoring the frequency of these manifestations, in forums all-encompassing and broad enough to represent a proxy of the collective psychological environment, both the conscious and unconscious, one can observe and distinguish the active archetypes for the dormant ones.

The Jungian theory holds that archetypes start to activate as part of a mechanism to ensure the holistic mental balance of a mind that has become too restricted, withholding normal instincts and reactions, due to a repressive psychological environment. The activation of an archetype itself can, as part of its birth pangs, lead to excesses before it integrates with the conscious part of the mind. This could manifest as violent eruptions or, in the financial perspective, asset bubbles. The increase of archetype-related symbols give an indication of what archetype is starting to activate, for example, the archetype The Warrior would give rise to the use of war-like metaphors in non-war-like contexts. This takes place without people being aware or understanding why they suddenly start to use such vocabulary; it is seen only as another trend, impacting the thought patterns towards the direction of an aggressive perception of reality and eventually increasing the likelihood for more aggressive behaviour, including the way financial decisions are being made. Increased symbol occurrences can therefore be used as acting precursors between the time lag of the archetype-induced thought patterns and their associated behaviour, enabling the possibility of commercially exploitable forecasts in terms of investment activities.

Important to note is that the activation of a specific archetype leads to an increased probability of a certain behaviour, rather than a certainty, and one cannot exactly point to where its energy will manifest. However, studying previous historical activations of the particular archetype will provide clues on how it will play out.

Areas for Further Research

The most current findings in neuroscience, although not conclusive in nature yet, and noted similar phenomena well represented in other academic disciplines, though labeled differently, give every indication of the existence of archetypes, a sort of innate thought pattern residing in the unconscious that is activated to address psychological imbalances.

And although almost a century has passed since Jung introduced the concept of archetypes, it is an area that has lagged in terms of statistical testing as one approach to validate the archetype-symbol-behaviour link hypothesis, in particular from the collective perspective. Whereas access to data, in size and coverage broad enough to represent the general, broader mindset were available back in Jung's days, the practical difficulties with manually collating and categorising such multifaceted data were significant enough to hamper any efforts to conduct empirical testing on that scale. The focus for research on archetypes and their manifestations had from the pragmatic point to be aimed towards individual patients and their relations to the unconscious and its symbolism, especially from the perspective of mental ailments. Aggregating the results from these individual studies, the researchers of the day could find common patterns in terms of recurring archetypes and symbols and draw inferences on commonalities in behavioural patterns. Jung and post-Jungians pointed to the possibility of tracking archetypal energies in the collective unconscious through symbols, and it is this fundamental assumption that underpins the research and testing that this book is based on. And with straightforward access to big data (rather than having to go through the burdensome task of sampling data from individuals and dealing with problems of subjectivity) the big data approach provides a more objective, holistic way to study symbolism and ensures frequent updates that, with appropriate categorisation, can help to form the time series, thus enabling statistical testing.

Whilst reviewing symbols and their potential influence on investment behaviour through a statistical approach, a number of practical questions as well as questions of a philosophical disposition arise, which fall outside the scope of this book. To better understand the nature of archetypes and ultimately prove the validity of symbolic language's connection with the unconscious and its potential capability to act as precursors to recurring behaviour, attempting to answer those questions will help to advance this pioneering research area.

Time Constants

Is it possible to define constants between the time lag from the inception of an increasing trend of archetypal symbols and its corresponding reflections in the financial markets? In other words, is it possible to pin down a fixed range of time between the increase in frequency of a set theme of symbols and a particular move? For example, is there a repeated notable increase or decrease in price for a particular asset for a particular duration, such as if a theme of war-like symbols appears and within the time span of three to four weeks, while the price of gold increases at least 20 percent over the next three months? Furthermore, can this be forecasted with a high probability based on earlier occurrences? Being able to establish such constants would provide further confirmation of the hypothesis of the influence of symbols on specific behaviours.

As part of this review, one also needs to determine whether such constants would be of a universal character in that they would apply to all specific archetypes and specific financial assets or whether they would have to be defined individually. The generic mechanisms that trigger archetypes and their standardised features, such as archetypal images and symbols, would as a starting assumption point to a suite of generic constants that can be statistically confirmed only through more extensive testing.

Multiple Archetypes

Are the constraints of the mind such that only one archetype can be active at a time or is it possible that several archetypes can be active in parallel, with different strengths and with different time intervals? Jung pointed to the fact that individual personal complexes can be in conflict with reigning archetypes of the collective unconscious, which points at least to the possibility of the latter assumption. However, at the level of the collective unconscious, archetypes tend to activate aligned with particular cultural spheres. American or Western culture can be contrasted to that of Chinese culture and symbolism or that of Hindu culture and symbolism with differing psychological environments and the prospective need for specific archetypes. How such distinctively culturally regulated archetypes can be active in parallel and can interact or are doomed to conflict and with what associated behavioural consequences is an open question.

Adding to this query, one also needs to consider whether archetypes stay active only within a fixed set of time and then recede or whether this time frame differs depending on the psychological environment it is set to rectify. The particular study this book is based upon has focused only on symbol data included from the inception of the millennia onwards. This cut-off point was set due to difficulties in ensuring access to an all-encompassing media coverage from earlier dates. This constraint forced the study of archetypal influences to be limited to the short and medium term. Although the perspective of monthly and annual trends in the financial markets might suffice for a first review, trends stretching over decades are well recognised and, with access to financial data going back more than a century for stock markets (and for certain commodities such as gold, several centuries), extending the testing over a longer period would facilitate the understanding of archetypes and possibly help answer the question about multiple archetypes being active at the same time.

With such test data at hand, it could also be possible to determine if there are activated archetypes nested within each other; in other words, could there be shorter-term archetypes that activate within decade- or even century-long archetypes? If so, how will that affect performance if they are contrasting or even conflicting in nature, or does the very set-up of archetypes prohibit the possibility of such scenarios? Another hypothetical query to test is the possibility of archetypes on top of archetypes; instead of being conflicting, additional archetypes may activate in a way to help reinforce and exacerbate a particular trend. As such, they become part of a bigger narrative or saga playing out, in which individual archetypes are connected to one another through that narrative as well as by the timing of their activation. If so, once one has been able to determine the sequence of events for the particular narrative, it would then be possible to forecast the next archetype in line for activation and possibly also its timing.

Tipping Points

Even with a broad understanding of why archetypes activate, due to issues with imbalances in the mind that need to be rectified or to equip the mind with adequate thought patterns to respond to an emerging psychological environment, we need to know the exact levels that trigger activation. In other words, what is the tipping point? If such tipping points can be established and conceived beforehand, would that make it possible to anticipate when and possibly which archetypes are likely to trigger? Understanding to what heights the psychological environment needs to reach until the collective mental balance gets so out of tilt and hits a tipping point that an archetype needs to be activated could be determined by studying historical situations that have prompted archetypes, which could help pin down common denominators of such an environment, whether in the form of particular symbolism or actual manifestations.

Once an archetype becomes active, how exactly do the symbol formations spread throughout the collective and act as a signal to initiate a change in behaviour? Is it possible to model the spread of the symbols by using a similar approach to that of the spread of epidemics with particular tipping points, or by following Richard Dawkins's memetic process in the distribution of cultural ideas and information transfers?

If such an approach is possible, can then precursors of precursors be developed? Are there recurring patterns that portend adoption of an emerging theme of symbolic language that represents an awakening archetype? Could there also be commonalities in terms of pinning down what sources, categories, and even geographical locations act as the avant-garde symbolism of early adopters?

Subliminal Stimulation

Jung claimed that archetypes were autonomous, that they operate outside the influences of the conscious. Does that fact alone make it impossible to willfully trigger a particular archetype? If not directly possible, could a trigger of an archetype be forced through the deliberate causation of a psychological imbalance, or are there other ways to impact archetypes' energy levels? However, important to note is that the triggering of an archetype increases only the probability of certain collective behaviour occurring, rather than providing certainty of any outcomes. As highlighted in previous chapters, some empirical testing has shown that parts of the unconscious can be influenced.

If the likelihood of predetermined scenarios playing out exists as a possible trajectory through time, such as the creation of a price bubble for a particular financial asset, it can only eventuate if certain psychological triggers are given and escalate to breach set tipping points, so that the correct psychological set-ups are in place at the right time. To materialise such a "prophecy" would make sure on a collective level that the conscious psychological environment can to some degree be dictated and then with some level of probability anticipate the release of new thought structures that launch a different perception of reality.

If one understands what archetype has activated, it should be possible to speed up its development through acts that are aligned with the zeitgeist and direct that influence through symbols that correspond to the zeitgeist. If it is possible to establish what type of symbols will grip the masses unconsciously, and apply these symbols to promote (financial) products or political views to tilt public sympathy in its favour, these symbols should grip the general public unconsciously. Although archetypal influences increase the probability for certain behaviours, it is the way they play out that can never be pinned down. It will depend on cultural context and time epoch, which becomes less of a problem with regards to financial markets, as financial bubbles tend to follow the same phases even if the duration might differ somewhat in the bubble formation.

Archetypal Influences in Other Areas

Archetypes will impact not only financial markets but any other area of collective behaviour that is trending in nature and depends on human sentiments; this would include politics, consumer patterns, fashion, societal values and norms, crime rates, social unrest leading to riots and revolutions, and decisions to go to war.

Generally, trends in these areas are of a longer term than those in financial markets and some of them are harder to objectively register; in some cases it is not possible to record in the form of time series, rendering statistical analysis less applicable. How would one objectively categorise and time trends in fashion? For example, when exactly did the colour red start to be fashionable and when did it end and to what intensity, more so than previous colours?

Even areas such as crime rates that could easily be recorded and tracked through statistics have measurement problems that need to be recognised and adjusted. There are always a number of unreported crimes that will not be included in the statistics and it is not certain that the relationship between reported and unreported crimes remains constant over the measurement period, which risks of the distortion of trends. What constitutes a crime, for example, whether prostitution or certain tax-related issues are considered illegal, can also vary over time. Even murder and its historical trends need to be adjusted due to improved emergency rescue techniques that today save more lives than they did a few decades ago and thus distort the true murder rates. Studying dominant political movements over extended time periods also comes with challenges, regardless of democratic or authoritarian forms of government, as political manifestos and platforms can fluctuate drastically over time, even within the same political party. The ruling Communist Party of

China has, since its time in power in 1949, made considerable changes to its doctrine and the way it governs China, including a phase of radical cultural revolution to a currently more market-focused approach, that is, "socialism with Chinese characters."

These are merely a few examples of the difficulties in applying a statistical correlation approach in testing the time series of symbolic language with societal areas that can be indexed only partly. So studying archetypal influences in these areas comes with significant issues of subjectivity that need to be considered as well as distortion in data due to changing circumstances, with the consequence that the testing criteria and conditions of the empirical study might lead to shifting outcomes depending on the setup. For financial assets this is less of a problem, as data is frequently provided and readily available; it is exact in terms of values and its definition lacks ambiguities and subjective interpretations and there are generally few, if any, distortions in terms of scope over time that require adjustment.

Despite the lack of precision in assessing impacts of areas outside the financial markets, studies of prospective archetypal influence in these areas still have value. Admittedly, the existing models have limited capacity to forecast events such as civil unrest or war, which the "Arab spring," among others, has proven in recent years. For example, the study of intensified rhetoric leading up to political crises or revolutionary moods, applied through an archetypal symbolic approach, could have merits.

Accepting the possibility of archetypal influences as a driver for behaviour could possibly help explain seemingly unforeseen societal trends that according to existing models fall out of the expected path and puzzle academics. Such an example is the unexplained rise in crime levels not traditionally linked with a downtrend in the economy or an increase in crime among a certain demographic of the population.

Archetypal Influences in Other Cultures and Languages

The focus of this book has been exclusively on the appearance of archetypes in an American and Western cultural context and the symbol measurements confined to English-speaking media, albeit not solely US-centered but global in coverage and distribution, and its links to trends in primarily US-based financial assets. Nevertheless, applying only a Western-based cultural archetypal context onto these US-related financial assets will serve as a reasonable proxy for the dominating psychological sphere for the mindsets that provide perceptions in terms of valuations. For stock markets in other geographical regions, that is no longer the case; for example, in the Chinese stock markets, investor perceptions will to a large degree be based on Chinese cultural perceptions, mirrored through Chinese language symbolism.

Even if archetypes are universal in form, their content is unique depending on the dominating cultural settings for the society in which they appear, so a direct translation of symbolic language from English to Chinese is not possible, as specific idiosyncratic cultural components need to be factored in. In the Chinese example, influences from the Taoist religion and tradition, doctrines from Confucius, and the history of Chinese characters is unlike those of the Roman alphabet, partly assembled from root pictograms that were formed to create meaning, which provides additional symbolic features that can get lost in translation and needs to be considered. Attaching figurative language in Chinese, or indeed any other language, to universal archetypes in order to track trending symbolism in Chinese media needs to be a separate exercise from studying English language symbolism.

Are the Collective Unconscious and Its Archetypes Constraining Free Will?

If psychological forces we are not aware of influence our perception of the world and, in extension, the decisions we make based on these perceptions, is this a constraint of free will?

The study of the unconscious takes on perhaps the most important question over the past century, with implications not only in philosophy but also areas such as politics and law: whether there is a free will, or a nature versus nurture model. Are we born with a blank slate, *tabula rasa*, or do we have innate patterns that predispose, but do not dictate us, towards certain behaviours of which we are not aware, under specific psychological circumstances?

Intuitively we might say that unconsciously driven decisions are not made freely, nor are they free to a lesser degree than are conscious decisions. We tend to think that only conscious decisions can be called free, because only these involve reasoning processes of which we are aware and which we can influence, in other words, rational thinking. As rational thinking occurs in the conscious part of the mind and can be altered by us, should then unconscious decisions be likened to instinctual forces that come in force when certain catalysts are triggered, ensuring that we harmonise with a holistic psychological balance, not unlike the mating instinct to ensure the survival of the human race?

Are these mechanisms put in place to ensure—even if we cannot consciously understand them or they might bring with them seemingly less desirable displays—the activation of an archetype of aggressive nature to address a psychological environment that has become too docile and lethargic for long-term survival, where an increased level of violence might be regarded as "collateral damage" as part of a path towards a more sustainable psychological balance?

But recognising the influences the unconscious, understanding the reigning taboos contemporary society requires us to repress and their place in the psychological context, historically as well as currently, and bringing them to awareness, will help reduce the risk of creating a neurotic society that eventually can cause collateral damage manifesting as asset price bubbles.

Influences on Finance

The conformist economic theory, underpinned by the rational man foundation, has come to its proverbial end of the road, a fact reinforced by recent years' financial bubbles which economists have been at a loss to explain and failed to adhere to the rational man theorem. There is an acceptance of other forces at work, labeled *animal spirits, Mr. Market,* or something similar. However, they have not yet found their way into an academic framework and are generally regarded as "error terms" that seemingly just happen and explain why conventional theories are so lackluster in forecasting capabilities.

The sticking point in building a theoretical framework reflecting collective human behaviour, whether related to economics or other societal displays, is whether humans are always acting rationally or whether humans shift between rational and irrational behaviour. Or is it that humans are always rational but that the changing psychological environment, or zeitgeist, constraints that rationality by the boundaries it sets?

In the height of the zeitgeist, behaviour that once would be considered bizarre, even deranged, is seen as perfectly rational within those specific constraints of perceiving reality. Rationality has been adjusted to fit the zeitgeist's constraints, and in hindsight the bizarre behaviour is not only recognised but rewarded and reinforced as the psychological environment of society organises around it as well.

To be able to understand and factor the contemporary zeitgeist into a model framework helps to view reality and rational action without constraints.

Could the collective unconscious and its archetypes be the error terms that distort the assumptions of rationality that form the conformist economic theories? If yes, the path to an economic theory that better reflects reality will be the one that allows for regime shifts in the rationality assumptions, incorporating and taking guidance from the activated archetypes, representing the zeitgeist that influences and suppresses the options of investor preferences. Correctly calibrated, it would enable a model that is dynamic enough to reflect the psychic realities that drive investment decisions and also provide pointers, in advance, on when shifts in preferences are likely to occur.

Assuming archetypes as drivers behind the seemingly irrational behaviours holds certain merit as the phases of the atypical financial bubble do share many of the archetypal symptoms Jung described, although he never referred to financial markets. Archetypal thought patterns seem to be the glue to keep crowds together, a set of shared attitudes aligning with the convergence theory rather than the contagion theory.

Developing a time series of symbols related to specific archetypes from media sources, now greatly facilitated through the relatively easily available access to big data, a testing possibility hardly practically available in Jung's days, gives the opportunity to run correlation tests over extended time periods against the price trends of financial assets, rather than relying on case studies and anecdotal reviews. Testing archetypal influences on the financial markets has a benefit in that the abundant and easy access to data statistical testing and ranking of correlations provides objectivity rather than the approach of subjectively assessing the psychological environment on the political and cultural spheres, as there are few objective indicators that can gauge degree and direction of current trends unlike in financial markets.

However, a methodology problem in this approach consists of the relatively few natural links between archetypes and specific financial assets, exceptions being gold, silver, and risk averse and risk aggressive investments. Thus some of its relations will come through reverse engineering by backtesting symbols and evidencing historically high correlations between the symbol's noise-spike patterns and the asset's specific price trends, whether up or down. And although it is intriguing when repeated patterns are detected in the time series providing leading correlations, the risk for nonsense correlation becomes obvious. Addressing such concerns requires comprehensive testing through establishing composite indexes. By demanding a cluster of thematic symbols rather than a single symbol word to correlate in tandem with the financial asset helps to reduce the likelihood of random correlations and, to some extent, takes chance out of the calculation. Also, establishing the fact that the patterns of symbol eruptions into the conscious follows similar patterns, agnostic of word and over time, points to something more than just random patterns as does the generic lead time between symbol signals and the start of a price trend.

If repeated predictive correlation can be evidenced between symbols dedicated to a certain archetype and the expected behaviour materialises within a recurring time range, and random symbol words cannot produce similar correlation, this provides at least correlative support to the hypothesis of archetypal influence on behaviour, measured through it symbolic proxies.

The aim of this book has been to provide a first attempt at a methodology on how the collective unconscious influences human behaviour, demonstrated through investment decisions in the financial markets, highlighting how archetypes can give rise to financial bubbles. With the recognition of this being a frontier science, despite archetypes being a century-old concept, and hinging on conclusive neuroscientific support in the research of the mind and brain, correlation testing does provide certain endorsements to the theory and will help evolve it further, pointing to new directions. The book's aligned website, forecastrix.com, provides recent insights and updates, including archetypal indexes that aim to predict trends in major financial indexes.

About the Author

Niklas Hageback has extensive experience in the financial sector working at tier-one financial institutions and consulting firms, such as Deutsche Bank, KPMG, and Goldman Sachs, holding regional risk management and oversight roles in both Europe and Asia. His roles include leading the implementation of operational risk and economic capital frameworks as well as engaging in the public debate through writing articles, giving presentations, and participating in regulatory lobbying.

He currently resides in Hong Kong where he runs a money management firm and manages a portfolio of financial software start-up firms with a special focus on research and product development in the area of behavioural finance.

Index